COFFEE WITH THE PROPHET

A 21st Century Encounter with the Prophet of Islam

BY MARK A. GABRIEL

Former Lecturer of Islamic History at Al-Azhar University

Coffee with the Prophet
by Mark A. Gabriel, PhD
Published by Gabriel Publishing
P. O. Box 181974
Casselberry, FL 32718
USA
www.gabrielpublishing.org
www.coffeewiththeprophet.com

Unless otherwise noted, all quotations from the Quran are from *The Quran Translation*, 7th edition, translated by Abdullah Yusef Ali (Elmhurst, NY: Tahrike Tarsile Quran, Inc., 2001).

Quotations from the Quran marked Muhsin Khan are from *The Noble Quran*, translated by Muhammad Taqi-ud-Din al-Hilali and Muhammad Muhsin Khan (Medina, Saudi Arabia: King Fahd, 1988).

Quotations from the Quran marked Shakir are from the electronically scanned versions of M. H. Shakir's *English translation of the Holy Quran* (Elmhurst, NY: Tahrike Tarsile Quran, Inc.).

ISBN-13: 978-0-61520-728-5
Library of Congress Control Number: 2008938056

First Edition
08 09 10 11 12 — 9 8 7 6 5 4 3 2 1
Printed in the United States of America

Dedicated to Naguib Mahfouz

(1912–2006)

Winner of the 1988 Nobel Prize in Literature

Dr. Mahfouz, I miss your joyful, intellectual meetings at the Rish Coffee Shop in the center of Cairo. The words you said one night are still ringing in my ears. You encouraged us:

> Write! Don't fear the religious taboos, which are the reason for our nation's backward living. Our nation has used the past to create a giant prison, and we are the prisoners locked in it. Be like birds; turn your pens into wings and fly with our people into the sky of religious freedom.

Dr. Mahfouz, I cannot have coffee with you anymore, but I think that *Coffee with the Prophet* would make you proud. I am answering your challenge to turn my pen into a wing, and I am flying into the sky of religious freedom. I am praying not just for my people but for the whole world to fly with me.

Your student in literature,
Mark A. Gabriel

Contents

Introduction

Coffee with the Prophet is a fictional story, but you're going to learn more about fact than fantasy in this book.

In this book you will meet an enigmatic character named Sheikh Ahmed, who befriends Mustafa, a young lecturer at Al-Azhar University in Cairo. Sheikh Ahmed seems to be a simple tribesman, but Mustafa discovers that he has a much bigger agenda. I will not tell you at this point whether Sheikh Ahmed is really Muhammad, the Prophet of Islam, or not. You will discover that for yourself as you read the book.

However, when you hear Sheikh Ahmed speak, you hear the attitudes and opinions of Muhammad. And when you see Sheikh Ahmed on the cover of the book, you see a realistic picture of what Muhammad looked like. Through *Coffee with the Prophet*, you are going to experience what it would be like to walk and talk with Muhammad in the twenty-first century, just as he walked and talked with his companions in the seventh century.

The character of Sheikh Ahmed is based as closely as possible on how the Quran and Islamic history described Muhammad. If you want to see these sources, read the Notes section in the back of the book. It is organized by chapter and will give you the original sources from Islamic history, often including the direct quote and the website where you can read the entire passage in English for yourself.

Just as Sheikh Ahmed is based on Muhammad, the character of Mustafa is based on my life twenty years ago when I was a lecturer at Al-Azhar. For the safety and privacy of the people from my past, all character names are fictional, including names of family, friends, and professors at Al-Azhar. The only non-fictional names in the book are public figures (like Naguib Mahfouz) or figures from Islamic history. In fact, in this story I have also changed the location of my family home and the number of siblings in order to keep their identities secret.

You've heard the saying, "Truth is stranger than fiction." If you would like to know more about the personal experiences in my life that contributed to Mustafa's story, see the Notes section. The Notes will also tell you about news events that are included in the story, such as the woman who was arrested at Starbucks or the Muslim convert who was protected by the Pope.

Some terms that I use may be unfamiliar to you, so I have also included a glossary with words such as surah (chapter), hadith, *hajj, burqa*, and so on. When I quote from the Quran I usually use the English translation of Yusuf Ali. If I quote from a different translation, such as Muhsin Khan or Shakir, I will put the name of the translator next to the reference.

Finally, I want to address some issues that may cause people to unfairly criticize or condemn this book. As one who lived in Muslim society for thirty-four years, I realize that the nature of this book may cause some controversy. I am going to explain these issues now before they become overly exaggerated.

The Image on the Book Cover

First, let's consider the image on the cover. Some people may say, "Are you deliberately trying to provoke Muslims by using this picture? Don't you know that Muslims consider it blasphemy to make a drawing of Muhammad?"

First of all, there is not a specific verse in the Quran or hadith (stories from the life of Muhammad) that condemns making an image of Muhammad. The Quran, which has the highest authority in Islamic law, emphasizes that images are wrong when they are used as idols, but the Quran does not condemn images in general.

A ban on drawings in general comes from Muhammad's words in the hadith. Muhammad said, "All painters who make pictures would be in the fire of Hell...If you have to do it at all, then paint the pictures of trees and lifeless things..." (See Notes for the complete quote.) In other words, Muhammad prohibited making images of people and animals. Sunni Muslims accept this hadith, but Shia Muslims reject it because it originated with Aisha, one of Muhammad's wives, and Shia reject all hadith from her. Therefore, Shia history includes some drawings of Muhammad and his companions. In addition, at different times in history, Sunni Muslims ignored this hadith and also made drawings of people, including Muhammad, especially during the Ottoman Empire. The bottom line is that drawing an image of Muhammad is not at all universally condemned in the Muslim world.

I am not trying to provoke Muslims by using this image. I simply want to show what Islamic history says about the appearance of Muhammad. Most people don't realize that the hadith describe Muhammad's height, hair, clothes, shoes, face, hands, feet, and jewelry. (For more information, see the Notes section). My purpose is to present factual information.

If you write a book about trees, you put a tree on the cover. If you write a book about Muhammad, you put Muhammad on the cover.

Insulting Muhammad

The real issue is not about making an image of Muhammad; it is about insulting Muhammad. In 2005 a newspaper in Denmark printed twelve cartoons that criticized Muhammad. One showed Muhammad with a turban on his head that looked like a bomb with a lit fuse. After imams printed these cartoons and waved them in front of the Muslims at their mosques, the Muslim world erupted with anger. Hundreds of thousands of people rioted. Products from Denmark were boycotted. Danish embassies were attacked and Danish flags burned.

The Muslim world was not necessarily protesting the image; it was protesting the insult. Therefore, I want to point out emphatically that the image on the cover of this book is not insulting or offensive in any way. In fact, it is a professional and accurate depiction of what Muhammad looked like based on information from the best Muslim sources. This image should not cause any more reaction in the Muslim world than the many other historical drawings of Muhammad that are reproduced in textbooks and on the internet every day.

Freedom of Speech

I have one final reason for using the representation of Muhammad on the cover of this book. I strongly believe that the free world must not practice self-censorship in the face of threats and intimidation from any group in the world, including Muslims. Free people must not limit their human rights because of those who want to take human rights away. Freedom of speech is worthless if it is not exercised.

Coffee with the Prophet celebrates the freedom that all human beings deserve: the freedom to think.

Chapter 1

I Am a *Hafiz*

I am a *hafiz*. If you know the meaning of that word, then you already know a lot about me. A *hafiz* is a person who has memorized the Quran, and I became a *hafiz* when I was twelve. From then on I was known as Mustafa the *Hafiz*. Even adults greeted me with respect in our neighborhood, and during the holy month of Ramadan I had my special place in the mosque where each day I would recite one-thirtieth of the Quran so that I would finish the entire book by the day the fast ended.

My family was deeply committed to Islam. My father never missed a prayer time, even when he was sick. I remember one time he had kidney stones, and he was doubled over in pain, but he went to the dawn prayer before he finally agreed to go to the hospital. He owned a furniture factory and was known for his generosity in giving to the poor. At the end of Ramadan month, when the fast was broken, he would pay for huge feasts for the poor people of our community. He treated my mother with great respect, and he never married any more wives, even though Egyptian law permitted him to marry up to four at one time.

My mother was not well-educated, but she was absolutely committed to being a good Muslim wife and mother. She was so careful to cover her hair completely with her veil—even at home—that I was in my twenties before I saw her hair for the first time. She devoted her life to cooking, cleaning, and caring for us kids, and she did it with a smile. She loved to talk and ask me questions about what I learned at school. She was so proud of me.

I had two brothers and one sister. My older brother, Ibrahim, worked closely with my father and would some day take over the business. He and his wife and two kids lived in an apartment on the third floor of my father's house. Hoda, my sister, had married and lived with her husband just four houses away from my father's house. Hoda was always visiting my mother at our house and cooking meals with her in the kitchen. They liked to ask me questions about what I was learning in school. Finally, my best friend at home was my younger brother, Sayid. From the time we were children, we spent all our free time together. He was outgoing and full of energy, always ready to play soccer or take a swim in the river. He didn't like school, so he went to work for my father as soon as he graduated from high school. He was the only one in the family who was ever careless about the duties of Islam. "I'm just not a morning person," he would say sleepily when he missed a dawn prayer. "I'll be there tomorrow." When he was a child, he would sneak candy during the Ramadan fast.

There was one important difference between my brothers, my sister, and me. My parents sent them to the public school run by the government, but from the time I was four years old, my parents sent me to Al-Azhar religious school. After finishing the primary school, I continued with Al-Azhar high school, where the focus of my education was practicing the Quran and the teachings of Islam. Whatever we were studying, we memorized, including books full of stories about Muhammad. I sometimes wondered why I was the only one of my family who was singled out for a religious education.

As a teenager, I was proud of what I knew, and I was proud of who I was. I was proud that neighbors came to me when they had a question about Islamic history, or the life of Muhammad, or specific requirements for prayer or washing. Most of all I was proud of my religion and my performance of it. I was at the top of the world, and everyone else was beneath me. I did what was right, and I had no doubt about it. My name Mustafa meant "chosen one," and I felt I deserved that title.

I've tried to figure out when my feelings changed. I think it was when I started asking questions. In primary school and high school, we could ask, "What is the assignment?" or "When is the test?" But rarely did we have the opportunity to ask questions about what we were learning. I remember one time when we were learning about Paradise and the teacher told us that martyrs would receive seventy-two virgins as a reward. I asked, "Isn't that too many for one person?" My teacher glared at me, "Stupid boy. Allah gives the strength to those he rewards."

In high school, our lessons focused on the victories of Islamic history, how Muhammad and his followers defeated their enemies and expanded the empire. Teachers told us which stories to read and what they meant. At the university, I could read the histories for myself, and I didn't see the glorious picture that was presented to me in high school. I saw Muslims fighting and deceiving and murdering one another. Muhammad's closest companions treated his family with contempt after he died. A river of blood ran through the history of Islam, from the beginning to the present day. It was an ugly picture.

I struggled to understand. Were this chaos and bloodshed a deviation from Islam, or were they a result of it? I thought about the life of the Prophet. When he first received his revelations in Mecca, he focused on preaching. After he immigrated to Medina, he became a military leader, and one of his acts was to order an attack against a large caravan from the city of Mecca, which had rejected him. Until his death, he was busy leading raids, sending out military expeditions, and negotiating treaties with those who surrendered to him. Muhammad was responsible for the deaths of thousands—both Muslims and non-Muslims.

Muhammad's goal was always to protect Islam and make it more powerful. If it meant killing all the men of a village, he would do it. If it meant assassinating a poet, he would do it. Muhammad said Allah's angels fought alongside his military. So the bloody reigns of his successors should be no surprise.

During one class at the university, I asked the professor, "Why is it that you teach us all the time about jihad? What about the other verses in the Quran that talk about peace, love, and forgiveness?"

Immediately his face turned red with anger. "My brother," he said, "there is a whole chapter in the Quran called 'Spoils of War.' There is no chapter called 'Peace.' Jihad and killing are the head of Islam. If you take them out, you cut off the head of Islam."

Why would the God of heaven need people to fight for him? I thought. It just doesn't make sense. If he is all-powerful, he can fight for himself.

I also started to wonder about the duties of Islam. Why did we pray five times a day? Why not three or seven? How are my five prayers helping Allah or even helping me? I'm just repeating the same words over and over. I applied the same logic to the Ramadan fast. For one month of the year, Muslims did not eat or drink during daylight hours. What was the purpose of this? We were supposed to go deeper in faith, but I only saw people being tired and hungry and irritable with each other.

Even though I did all the duties day after day and year after year, I was on the brink of losing my faith, and I couldn't talk with anyone about it. If I asked these questions out loud, people would think that I was doubting my faith. I would bring shame on my family, and I would get in big trouble with the leaders of Al-Azhar, where critical questions were absolutely forbidden. If someone like me ever left Islam, his blood would be free. Any Muslim could kill him because the punishment for leaving Islam is death. His own family members would probably be the first ones to try to kill him.

When I led prayers at the mosque or recited chapters of the

Quran, it felt as if I were throwing sand in the wind. All my efforts were blowing away. I kept reaching out, trying to touch Allah, but I never felt him reaching back toward me.

I thought longingly of the time when I was a child and innocently wanted to be just like Muhammad. I wondered what it would be like to talk to Muhammad today. Would he be able to answer my questions and take away my doubt? I wished that I could go back in time to walk with the apostle of Allah, to hear his teachings firsthand so that I could be sure I was doing the duties correctly. Or perhaps Muhammad could come to me in a vision or dream to answer my questions. At every prayer time, I would plead, "Allah, lead me to the truth. Take away my doubts. Show me how you desire to be served."

I was essentially trapped at Al-Azhar. If I had been studying any other subject, like medicine or engineering, and realized that I did not like that subject, I could just change to a different one. But this was my faith, the foundation of my life. I couldn't stop and say, "I'm not interested anymore. I don't think I believe in what I'm doing."

So I kept taking classes—actually, I did more than take the classes. My family and friends will tell you that I never do anything halfway. So I excelled. I was second in my class when I graduated with my bachelor's degree. For my master's degree, I wrote a thesis that was so popular I was invited to read it on Egyptian public radio. My thesis argued that an Islamic government could be based on a consensus of opinion from among the people, which was my way of saying that Islam allowed democracy. However, radical groups hate the idea of democracy, declaring that democracy is not the truth of Allah but an invention of infidels, the impermissable substitution of man's law for that of Allah. At the age of thirty, I became the second youngest person to lecture for Al-Azhar University. I earned my doctorate two years later.

By the age of thirty-three, I was nearly a celebrity in Islamic scholarship—and I was on the brink of abandoning my faith. I couldn't talk with anyone about what I was feeling, especially my family. I couldn't bear to disappoint them that way. Even worse, if anyone thought that I had left Islam, my life would be in danger. Anyone could kill me because Islamic law states that the one who leaves Islam shall be killed.

I probably would have walked this tightrope for the rest of my life except for a letter I received from the university three weeks after I graduated in the spring of 2008. The letter read, "Congratulations on your acceptance to the faculty of the School of Arabic Language. In honor of your achievement and to prepare you for service to the Muslim community, the university has secured a reservation for you to fulfill the duties of the *hajj* this year in August 2008."

Is this how Allah is answering my prayers? I wondered. If I go to the land where Islam began, maybe I will understand Islam better. Maybe Allah will give me a sign that I am pleasing him. A month later I was in a plane on my way to Saudi Arabia to perform one of a Muslim's greatest acts of worship—the *hajj.*

Every Muslim must try to do the *hajj*, or pilgrimage, to Mecca, Saudi Arabia, at least once in a lifetime. From the time I was a little boy, I dreamed of going to the *hajj.* Our teachers drilled us on the duties that must be performed. Most people would need to carry a handbook or follow a guide to do the rituals correctly. But I had them memorized.

I would join two million Muslims who would spend the same six days doing the same rituals—circling the Black Stone at Mecca, worshipping at Mount Arafat, throwing pebbles at Satan, shaving our heads, and slaughtering a lamb.

This is where my story begins. I was desperately seeking a sign from Allah during the *hajj*, but as you will see, the sign came to me in a most unexpected place.

The Holy Ground

I woke up before dawn and stared at the ceiling of the tiny tent where I had spent the night. *If Allah is going to send me a sign, this is the day*, I said to myself. *This may be the best chance I will have in my entire life*. It was the second day of the pilgrimage—the most holy day because all the pilgrims would gather to worship Allah at Mount Arafat where Muhammad gave his final sermon to the Muslim nation fourteen hundred years ago. Most people would stay in the plain, but my goal was to climb the mountain all the way to the place where Muhammad stood. I thought, *If I stand where the Prophet stood, Allah may notice me.*

I groped in the dark for a flashlight. It was 3:30 in the morning, but the heat kept my scalp damp with sweat. It was 90 degrees Fahrenheit (32 degrees Celsius) at night and could get up to 110 degrees Fahrenheit (43 degrees Celsius) during the day. I found a water bottle and drank it quickly. This was the most physically demanding day of the *hajj*. Most of us on the pilgrimage would not eat or drink again until sunset so that we could concentrate fully on Allah.

I checked my watch: I had thirty minutes before the call to prayer. Like all the other pilgrims, I was wearing a simple pair of white pants with a rope belt. I took a piece of white cloth and draped it over my shoulder and across my chest and back. Stepping outside my tiny tent, I gazed at the endless rows of white tents stretching out in front of me, glowing in the stadium lights. I would be sleeping in a tent for the next five days.

I hurried to one of the washing stations set up by the Saudi government and did the ritual washing required before prayer. After washing up to five times a day since I was five years old, I could do the washing in my sleep. If the Prophet were washing next to me that day, we would have been doing exactly the same thing because every detail of this washing was taken from his example.

I sat on a little bench in front of the spigots with my feet in front of me. As the water flowed, I first washed my right hand, then my left hand. Next I rinsed my mouth with water and then my nose. I used my hands to wipe water over my face. Then I washed my arms up to the elbows, wiped water over my hair, and used a wet finger to clean my ears. I finally ended by washing my feet, carefully cleaning between each toe.

With washing finished, I walked briskly back to my tent, sat down inside, and began reciting. The words of the Quran flowed over my tongue like water flowing in a brook. I had practiced them so many times that it almost felt as if my tongue was forming the sounds by itself. All I had to do was breathe them out.

That morning I recited *Surah al-Hajj* because I was fulfilling the sacred duties of *hajj* (Quran, chapter 22). With ten minutes before the first call to prayer, I began to chant praises to Allah. The loudspeakers outside came to life with a crackling sound followed by the smooth, undulating call to prayer. Minutes later, the rich voice on the loudspeaker led the prayer, blending more than two million individuals into one inseparable voice. I knelt on the simple rug in my tent, and I could hardly hear my own voice as it melted into the murmur of this sea of people. At the moment when I touched my forehead to the ground, I prayed desperately, "O Allah, hear the cry of your servant. Give me a sign today that I am pleasing you. Show me the right path."

When dawn prayers were done, I blended into a stream of humanity trudging through the burning desert sand toward the plain of

Arafat. I chanted in unison with the sweaty, jostling crowd around me, letting the rhythm of the Arabic words fill my mind:

> Here I am, O Allah. Here I am.
> You have no partner.
> Here I am.
> You alone deserve all praise and gratitude.
> To you belong all favors and blessing and sovereignty.
> And you have no partner.

For six miles we walked east through the desert, passing through the hills of Muzdalifah. When I finally saw the plain of Arafat in front of me, filling up with white robed pilgrims like a river behind a dam, waves of emotion crashed over me. *I'm almost there*, I thought. *This is my chance!*

Most of the people were exhausted from the heat and stopped to rest on the plain wherever they could. Many were praying urgently, with tears flowing from their eyes. Those who were strong and healthy tried to stay standing until sunset, just as Muhammad taught. Others rested on the ground briefly before standing up again.

I felt a burst of energy as I pushed past people in the plain, getting closer and closer to my goal—Mount Arafat, the Mount of Mercy. When Muhammad gave his farewell sermon to the Muslim community at the *hajj*, he stood on this hill. That is where I wanted to be on this holy day—to stand where Muhammad stood. Huge boulders dotted the sides of the hill, mixed with pilgrims already climbing to the top. My white clothes drenched in sweat, I chose one of the paths through the rocks and pressed upward.

My heart was beating faster and faster. When I could get no closer to the top because of the crowd, I turned around and looked down at the people in the plain. For a moment, I felt as if I were flying up to heaven, carried on the prayers of more than two million people, as they echoed between earth and sky. If I ever hoped to reach Allah, this was the day and the place. *Pray, Mustafa, pray!*

Don't miss your chance! The words throbbed in my head.

First I prayed for all the requests that my family and friends had given me. They trusted me to take them to the holy land, and I would never want to disappoint them. Then I cried out for myself. "Allah," I prayed, "I am your slave. I want to obey you. Give me a sign that I am pleasing you. Show me the right path. Show me the truth." I prayed for hours, with both hands raised in the air over my head. When my arms got tired, I would put them down for a few minutes but I raised them again as soon as I could.

Finally, my brain and body were exhausted. I collapsed onto the ground, shaking from hunger and thirst. All I could do was to listen to the chanting, and in that moment of weakness, my true thoughts broke into my consciousness. *Is this really the way we are supposed to communicate with Allah—suffering through the* hajj*—the fasting, the walking, the chanting, the prayer? Will the God who asked us to make the pilgrimage speak to our hearts or souls now?*

The chanting rose and fell. I began to notice that at the end of each chant there would be a moment before the next one began. And in that pause, there was a moment of silence—empty, terrible silence. The silence of heaven was louder than all the noise we were making on earth. I felt numb.

Where is he? Why am I doing this? I struggled to stand on my feet again.

The rest of the day was a blur to me. I followed the crowd down off the Mount of Mercy and through the plain of Arafat back to the hills of Muzdalifah, about two more miles of walking, where I would spend the night in another massive tent city. I did the last two prayers of the day in my tent. By this time, my throat felt as dry as the sand blowing around my feet. I recited several chapters of the Quran and finally decided that I needed to lie down. I was exhausted and weak, but sleep would not come. My mind kept going back to a story that had troubled me since I was twelve years old.

Family Secret

When I finished memorizing the Quran at the age of twelve, I wanted to do more than quote the Quran: I wanted to live it and handle the situations around me according to its words. At the same time, my teachers at Al-Azhar elementary school always told us how Islam is superior to all other religions. And they always warned us that Jews and Christians hate Muslims and want to destroy Islam. That is why I was so bothered by a tiny Christian church in the Christian neighborhood next to my neighborhood. A priest lived in a little house not far from the church. I looked at that church and that house, and I thought, *They have no right to live here next to us.*

One summer the priest went away for a month and left his little house empty. I told my younger brother, Sayid, who was nine years old at the time, "That priest is an enemy of Islam, and he shouldn't be living in our city. Let's teach him a lesson." I talked Sayid into sneaking out of our house one night after everyone was asleep. We gathered stones in the folds of our robes and crept through the dark streets to the priest's house. When we were in position across the street, I instructed Sayid, "Throw your stones at the windows as fast as you can and then run. Ready? Go!" We hurled stones at the house furiously, shattering every window within seconds. Lights snapped on, and neighbors came running out as we raced down the street back to our neighborhood.

We thought no one could identify us. We were wrong. The next day the Christians told my father what had happened, and he was furious with my brother and me. My father was a hardworking businessman with a good reputation in the community. He treated everyone around him with fairness—whether they were Muslim or Christian.

My dad gave us the beating of our lives that day, but I was defiant. In my mind, I was doing the right thing for Islam. At dinnertime, my mother brought us some bread and stew to eat in our rooms. I could see that she had been crying, but she said nothing about what happened.

The next day she came to me and said, "Mustafa, I am going to bake bread. Come with me." Normally, I loved to go with her to the outside oven where she would pinch off pieces from a huge dough ball and flatten them into little cakes to be baked. She was one of the few ladies left in our neighborhood who still baked bread the old-fashioned way. While she worked, she would ask me questions about school and my friends and always wanted to know what was going on in my life. This time my heart sank because I knew I had disappointed her. But my mother wasn't going to lecture me about what I had done. She wanted to tell me something about myself that I never knew before.

"Mustafa," she said, "there's something I should have told you a long time ago."

I was puzzled and asked, "What is that, Mother?"

As she pulled and shaped the dough, she quietly told the story. "When you were born, you cried all the time. I tried to nurse you, but within an hour after you ate, you would be screaming and crying. We tried formula from bottles, but nothing worked. You weren't gaining weight, and you cried constantly. I had my sister and two of my friends come to the house to try to nurse you, but you would not nurse from them. Not even the doctor knew what to do."

My mother stopped talking for a moment, and I could see the tears in her eyes. She pushed a tray full of dough cakes into the oven and then continued with the story.

"After two weeks, you finally stopped crying because you were so weak. You just lay still in my lap all night, and I cried over you. That morning one of our Christian neighbors, Umm William, came to our house and asked, 'How is little Mustafa?'

"I told her, 'He can't nurse. I don't know what to do.' Umm William had a six-month-old son that she was nursing, and she said, 'My dear Khadija, would you like me to try?'

"I put you in her lap, and as she held you close, I heard her whisper, 'In the name of Jesus.'

"'No,' I said, 'don't say that.' But then I stopped because you began to nurse, and I could see the milk dripping off your chin. And you nursed until you were full, and then you fell asleep in her arms. Umm William went home, and you did not wake up screaming and crying like you did before.

"Your father and I didn't know what to do. We didn't want you to be nursed by a Christian woman, but she was the only one you would take. So Umm William nursed you until you were able to eat solid food."

My mother had been sitting motionless, with a pinch of dough in her hand as she talked. She finally started rolling the dough into a ball again.

"No—I don't believe you..." I said.

She continued, "Your father and I did not know how you would be affected by nursing from a Christian woman. So your father asked his brother, your Uncle Hamzi, to help you memorize the Quran. The reason you've gone to the religious schools all your life is to protect your faith. Without Islam we are nothing. But the hatred in your heart toward Christians—Islam doesn't teach you to do this. That is why I wanted you to know this story."

I couldn't say anything for a long time. I pulled a pan of steaming pita loaves out of the oven and put them on a platter to cool.

"Do my brothers know?" I whispered.

"No," she answered. "They do not need to know."

"Mother," I said, "as Allah is my witness, I will never give up my faith, and I will not disappoint you again."

She hugged me through her tears.

I told myself, *I am not going to let Satan influence me by that Christian milk. I am going to serve Allah better than anyone else around me.*

These were the thoughts running through my mind as I tossed and turned in my little white tent in the holiest month of the year in the holiest place on earth.

I felt torn in two pieces. One side said, "Mustafa, resist the devil! He is able to attack you because you had a Christian mother in nursing. You must bring your thoughts under control if you want to please Allah."

The other side said, "Mustafa, this has nothing to do with what happened to you as a baby. This is about now. Where is God in all the rituals that you are doing now? Why did Allah tell Muhammad to do all these things?"

The exhaustion in my body finally conquered the turmoil in my brain, and I fell into a restless sleep. I had four more days of *hajj* to go.

Chapter 4

Stoning Satan

The next morning I felt somewhat better. *Maybe I was too tired and hungry yesterday*, I thought. *Satan was confusing me. Maybe Allah will give me a sign today.* I resolved to concentrate on my worship no matter what I felt.

The day before, I had collected seven pebbles from hills of Muzdalifah. I slipped them into my bag and, immediately after dawn prayers, set off with the crowds for the desert plain of Mina where we would do the ritual of stoning Satan. In the plain there were three huge concrete basins with a curved cement wall rising out of the center of each one. This is where we would stone Satan. Considering my thoughts from the day before, I was eager to take my stand against Satan. As I threw my seven pebbles at the largest concrete pillar, I shouted at the top of my voice, "The curse of Allah be upon you, Satan!" Pilgrims were throwing pebbles to my left and to my right, and they all clattered against the concrete monument endlessly. I felt nothing. The people behind me were pushing to make their way to the basin, so I walked away. *Remember*, I told myself, *your duty is to submit to Allah's will.*

I fulfilled my duties for that day meticulously. I stood in line and had my head shaved just as Muhammad commanded. This day of the *hajj* is known as *Eid al-Adha*, the day of remembering the ram that Abraham sacrificed in place of his son Ishmael. I bought my lamb and sacrificed it myself, just as I had seen my father do at home since I was a little child. The butcher tied the lamb's legs together and put the animal on its side. Then I put my knee on the lamb's body and held its head with my left hand. With my right hand I cut the lamb's throat, and the blood gushed onto sand that was already stained red. The animal quickly went limp.

I would never taste the meat of this lamb; the butcher would donate it to the poor. I didn't feel sorry for the lamb; when I was younger all of us kids loved this day because it meant we would have a lot of meat to eat. I thought about my family in Egypt, who would also be sacrificing a lamb that day and eating it together. I knew they would be talking about me and wondering how I was doing.

In the afternoon, I walked with the crowds the three miles back to Mecca and went to the Grand Mosque to do *tawaf*, which is to walk around al-Ka'aba seven times in a counterclockwise direction. Al-Ka'aba is a cube-shaped building in the courtyard of the Grand Mosque. It is about forty feet tall (twelve meters), constructed of granite bricks, and draped with a heavy black silk cloth with gold embroidery.

Tawaf is not a one-time event in the *hajj*. I had already performed *tawaf* on the first day of my *hajj*, and I would do it several times in the days to come. I think it was the repetition that made *tawaf* frustrating for me. I had to fight against my thoughts. *Why am I walking around a square building? I am not worshiping this stone. So what am I doing?*

I silenced those thoughts by remembering a story about Umar ibn al-Khattib, one of Muhammad's closest companions. Umar was performing *tawaf*, and he said to the Black Stone at al-Ka'aba: "You are just a stone. I know you are just a stone, and I would never kiss you except I saw the Prophet do it." So I controlled my doubts by thinking, *I must do this by faith, just as Umar did.*

That evening I walked the three miles back to the tent city of Mina, where I had slept on the second night of the *hajj*. I would sleep in this tent city until the *hajj* was over.

The next two days were exactly the same, except that I did not sacrifice any more lambs. But each day I threw stones at Satan in Mina and did *tawaf* around al-Ka'aba. The rest of the time I spent in prayer or reciting the Quran. I felt like a robot, going through motions decided by someone else.

I thought about how excited my family was that I could do the *hajj*. No one else in my family had ever gone—not even my father. Again I had been the chosen one, just as my name Mustafa meant. I knew they would be talking about me while I was gone and would be excited to hear me tell about what I had done.

I looked at the people around me, all faithfully performing the duties of the *hajj*. Many had saved money their entire lives to make this trip. Some of the elderly did not have the physical strength to walk around al-Ka'aba, so they would lie down inside long wooden boxes and young men would carry the box on their shoulders so they could do *tawaf*.

The summer heat was hard on everyone. During the day as I walked back and forth between Mecca and Mina, sweat poured off my body. Several times I saw medics carrying away a pilgrim who had collapsed from the heat. Sunstroke was a great danger when the *hajj* occurred during the summer, and dozens of people died each year.

I was relieved when I walked around al-Ka'aba one last time for the Farewell *Tawaf* and could go to my room at a little family hotel a few blocks outside of the Haram Gate in Mecca. I had left my luggage with them before I went on the pilgrimage, so it was waiting for me. I planned to spend one night in Mecca before taking a taxi or bus to Medina to see the grave of the Prophet and then flying home from Jeddah.

After I checked in, I realized that I hadn't eaten since early that morning, and it was already nearly 10:00 p.m. I showered and put on my regular clothing for the first time in nearly a week. Because I represented Al-Azhar, I tried to look proper whenever I was in public, so I put on a pair of suit pants with a dress shirt and a tie. Just before I left the room I picked up a notebook that I had brought with me. The university wanted me to teach a special seminar about the *hajj* after I returned, so I wanted to take some notes.

I stepped out of the lobby into the hot summer night and began to wander down the street. After a few blocks, I came to the Hilton Hotel, and I knew that a three-level mall was inside. These massive hotel/shopping areas were too commercial to be so close to al-Ka'aba, I thought. But I was hungry and tired, and I knew it would be easy to get something to eat inside. I ducked in, and the first place I saw was a coffee shop.

An Unexpected Companion

The air-conditioned interior of the mall was a huge relief from the heat outside. I quickly picked out a sandwich and asked for a cup of plain black coffee. This was one of those Western-style coffee shops with padded chairs and coffee tables. *Why not be comfortable for a change?* I thought, and sank down into a black leather chair.

I started to eat my sandwich and didn't pay any attention to the people going in and out of the shop. It was mostly men coming to get a cup of coffee and then continuing on their way. Sometimes a group of women would come in, covered from head to toe with black robes *(burqas)* and head scarves *(hijabs).* They would sit together in a booth, lifting the bottoms of their scarves so they could sip their lattes and cappuccinos. There were no men and women sitting together to talk, which didn't surprise me. Just a few months earlier the Saudi morality police had arrested and jailed a woman, who was fully covered, for sitting in a booth with a male co-worker who was not her husband. The woman and several men had been working at their offices near the coffee shop when the electricity went out. So they all went to the coffee shop to use the wireless internet connection and continue to work. For a second I wondered if Muhammad would have punished that woman if he had seen what she did. Ironically, women were serving the customers in the shop, working while covered in their *burqas. Would Muhammad allow that?* I wondered.

As I ate, I started to write some notes about my pilgrimage. No matter what I was thinking on the inside, I would have to be prepared to teach the seminar when I got home. I was so absorbed in my writing that I didn't notice a figure standing right in front of me. Finally, I heard him clear his throat and say, "Peace be upon you," in Arabic. Surprised, I looked up. Standing in front of me was a man who looked as if he had ridden a camel into the mall. He was wearing a dark brown robe of thick, coarse cloth and had a brown turban on his head. He had a full black beard with almost no hint of gray, and his black eyes sparkled underneath his heavy eyebrows.

"And also upon you," I responded, standing to my feet.

He had a large coffee cup in one hand and a rough brown bag slung over his shoulder. "Is this seat taken?" he asked in classical Arabic. He gestured toward the empty black leather chair next to me.

"No, it's not," I said. "I would be honored for you to join me."

This is amazing, I thought. *This man speaks the classical Arabic of the Quran, and he's dressed like someone from the pages of a history book. I wonder what sect he belongs to and why he has come to this coffee shop.*

No matter what sect he came from, I was honestly glad to have some company. Many people do the *hajj* in groups, but I had gone alone so that I could concentrate on Allah more fully. It turned out that my own thoughts were more of a distraction than a friend would have been. I liked the idea of talking with this man for a while. He seemed like the kind of person who would have strong opinions. He settled into the stuffed leather chair next to me and sighed comfortably.

"The *hajj* means discipline of the body, wouldn't you say so, my friend," he said smiling. "Have you come here for *hajj* and *umrah?*"

"I have been honored to perform them this year," I answered. "Have you come for the *hajj* as well?"

"I live in this area," he answered, "and I never miss *hajj*, *inshallah* [Allah willing]. When I climb Mount Arafat and see millions of Muslims gathered together on the plain below, I feel life flowing into my body. The whole world recognizes the power of the Muslim *ummah* when the people gather together at the *hajj*. May Allah hasten the day when the whole world is submitted to the law of Islam."

"I climbed the mountain too. There is nothing to compare to that moment," I agreed, trying hard to sound convincing. He watched me carefully as I spoke. He seemed to know that I did not say everything that I thought, but he wasn't going to push me for it. He looked at my notebook with curiosity. "What are you writing about?" he asked.

"I'm preparing for a seminar I'm going to teach," I answered. "I am a lecturer for Al-Azhar University in Cairo."

He clapped his hands. "Al-Azhar!" he exclaimed. "You must be a great scholar."

"It's my first year as a lecturer," I explained. "I just earned my doctorate."

"Even so," he said, "teaching is a great honor and responsibility. You are privileged that Allah chose you for this task."

"With Allah's help, I will do my best," I answered. I noticed that my companion had finished his coffee and was playing with a thick silver ring on his first finger. I thought his hands seemed unusually large for a man of average height, but I also thought perhaps the ring was affecting my perception.

I was so busy wondering about his ring and his clothing that I almost forgot my manners. According to traditional Arabic culture, the one who arrives first will pay for the food or drink and serve the other, so I said, "Sir, I see that you have finished your coffee. May I buy another one for you?"

"Thank you," he answered with a pleased look on his face.

"My favorite drink used to be milk from my herds—goats, sheep, or camels. But when I tasted my first latte, I felt like I was drinking from the rivers of Paradise. I drink one every chance I get. By the way—be sure to have it sweetened with honey, and pour it over ice. I need something to cool off on this hot summer evening."

As I went to the counter, I sneaked a look back at this intriguing stranger. *He must have quite a story behind his beard and his robe*, I thought. I also noticed that he was wearing an unusual pair of sandals. They looked almost handmade, held on with just two leather straps crisscrossed over the top of his feet. His feet seemed unusually large, like his hands. *Maybe the sandals make his feet look big*, I thought.

"Sir," I said, handing him the latte, "I will be teaching a seminar soon about the *hajj*. Since you are from this area, could you tell me about some of the historical places in Mecca and Medina? I would like to visit some of them tomorrow."

"My son," he answered, "I am sorry to say there is a big problem with that." I noticed a flash of anger in his eyes. "Do you know where Abu Bakr's home is?" He looked indignant. "We're sitting on it! They built this hotel and mall on top of it.

"Do you know what you will find if you go to the house of Muhammad's first wife, Khadija, where they lived together and their six children were born?" He paused and then said in a low growl, "Toilets. A public bathroom.

"The Prophet's birthplace has not even been spared. But at least there is a library there with books about Mecca and not rows of toilets!

"These people have no idea what the word *respect* means. The Prophet and his companions are not to be worshiped, but they must be given respect! Allah will deal with them on Judgment Day!"

He had not raised his voice, but he was speaking with intensity, and the other people in the coffee shop looked at us with curiosity. I wasn't sure if they heard what he was saying, but it seemed better to me not to fill too many ears with complaints about the

Saudi government. I admired his passion, though. *He speaks with the fervor of a true prophet*, I thought.

"You are right," I said. "This is a disgrace to the Muslim world. May Allah forgive us."

He nodded. "I am so glad that one like you is going to teach at Al-Azhar," he said. "We need more strong believers there who will not compromise the teachings of Islam."

"Sir," I asked, "are the historical sites in Medina gone as well? Tomorrow I will go to the Prophet's Mosque in Medina, and I wanted to see the historical sites there too."

He answered, "Many of those sites have disappeared too, but there are some that you can still visit. I am but a simple tribesman, but I have been in the area a long time, and I still know where the historical sites are."

I was curious to learn more about this stranger. "Would you be able to show me some of the historical sites in Medina?" I asked.

"By Allah," he replied, "you have a good idea." He picked up a rough cloth bag next to his chair and put the strap over his shoulder. "Let's go."

He has a lot of energy for someone who looks like he is in his sixties, I thought.

"Sir," I said, "I would like more than anything to go with you tonight, but my brain and body are too tired. Could we go tomorrow? I will get a car to drive to Medina."

"That would be fine," he answered graciously. "We can meet here at the coffee shop after dawn prayers." As we walked out together, I finally asked him a question that had been on the tip of my tongue all night. "What is your name, sir?" I asked.

"You can call me Sheikh Ahmed," he answered. "And what is your name?"

"Mustafa al-Rahal. I am from Egypt."

"Mustafa the Egyptian," he said, gazing directly into my eyes. "I look forward to seeing you tomorrow." He turned and walked toward the Grand Mosque, and I turned to go back to my hotel, wondering what the next day would bring. I looked back one time to make sure he was OK, but his figure had already disappeared in the shadows.

I couldn't explain why, but I looked forward to seeing Sheikh Ahmed in the morning.

I slept soundly that night, the first time in many days.

Chapter 6

Better than Camels

After dawn prayer the next morning, I hurried to the coffee shop. As soon as I opened the door, I saw him sitting there in the same leather chair he had occupied the night before. I greeted him according to Islamic tradition by saying, "Peace, mercy, and blessings be upon you from Allah."

He nodded and answered, "Peace, mercy, and blessings be upon you from Allah as well, Mustafa the Egyptian." He was wearing exactly the same clothing, but he looked refreshed. His beard was shining, and a pleasant scent of sandalwood hung around him. Hanging over one shoulder, he had the same rough cloth bag that he was carrying the night before.

"Before we go," he said, "let's have some coffee." Before I could answer, he was up at the counter, ordering two iced honey lattes. He came back with the drinks and sat down again. "Try this," he said with a glimmer in his eye. "I think you'll like it."

I took a sip and had to agree with him. The taste of honey in the latte was delicious. I asked, "Can you tell me about your family? Do you have any family living close to you?"

"All my wives died long ago," he said, "and I have no children left alive either. I used to live in Mecca, but I moved to Medina."

"Do you work in Medina?" I asked.

"Actually, I have a shop that sells supplies for the Bedouins who live in the desert. I don't spend much time there anymore because I have young people who take care of the shop. I like to travel and meet people. What about you?" he asked. "Are you married?"

"Sadly," I answered, "I have not made time to find a wife. I spent all my time studying to earn my doctorate degree from Al-Azhar. I live at my father's house just outside of Cairo." I glanced at my watch and noticed that it was already almost 8:00 a.m. "Are you ready to go now?" I asked. "It takes about four hours to drive to Medina, and I want to have enough time to see the sites."

"Of course," he replied, leaping to his feet. "Let's be on our way."

Driving in the rental car was a welcome change from trudging through the desert during the pilgrimage. It felt as if we were flying as the sand dunes and scraggly bushes slid past the car windows. One time we saw a group of Bedouins herding camels with a cloud of dust trailing after them. Sheikh Ahmed asked me, "Have you ever ridden the child of a she-camel?"

"I don't think so," I answered. "I'm much too big to ride the child of a she-camel."

"But my son," said Sheikh Ahmed, "do any others than she-camels give birth to camels?" He smiled so mischievously that I had to laugh.

"Seriously," he went on, "I much prefer to make this journey by car during the day than by camel at night."

I thought to myself, *Why would Sheikh Ahmed ride a camel at night from Mecca to Medina? That's a long way to sit on a camel when you could ride in a car. If Sheikh Ahmed really did ride a camel from Mecca to Medina, he would have followed in the footsteps of Muhammad and Abu Bakr fourteen hundred years earlier. They left Mecca at night on camels to establish a new headquarters for the*

Islamic movement in Medina. This event, known as the hijra, was so important that it is the beginning of the modern Islamic calendar.

I decided to try to find out more about Sheikh Ahmed. "Can I ask you a question?" I asked. "What sect do you belong to? Does everyone wear your kind of clothing and sandals?"

He answered, "I do not belong to a certain sect. I think one of the greatest tragedies of the Muslim world is how the believers are divided into so many different sects. Allah told the Muslims, 'And verily this *ummah* [the entire Islamic nation or community] of yours is a single *ummah* and I am your Lord, so keep your duty unto me. But they have broken their religion among them into sects, each sect rejoicing in its tenets' (Surah 23:52–53). But the Prophet knew that the divisions would come. He warned, 'My *ummah* will split into seventy-three sects: one will enter Paradise and seventy-two will enter hell.'"

I answered, "This hadith is very popular among scholars. They use it whenever there is a disagreement to argue that their sect is right and all the other sects are wrong. But how can a person be sure he is in the right sect?"

"My son, you have asked a very important question. Let us look to the words of the Prophet for the answer. He said, 'I left something with you, and if you take it and hold it, you will never be led astray. It is the book of Allah and the Prophet's example.' The Quran tells us that on Judgment Day, 'the unjust person will bite his hand and say I wish I followed the path of the Prophet.' So the ones in the right sect are the ones who follow the Quran and the Prophet most closely."

I nodded my head in agreement, but I thought to myself, *Every Muslim wants to follow the Quran and the Prophet. The problem is that Muslims can't agree on what the Quran means and what the Prophet said.* I decided not to tackle such a big question, but I still wanted to know about Sheikh Ahmed's clothes. I asked, "If you are not part of a certain sect, then how did you decide on the clothes that you wear?"

Sheikh Ahmed answered, "I wear these clothes because I'm used to them and they are the most comfortable for me. I have no problem with you wearing your modern pants and shirts either."

"I am glad to hear that," I said. Then a question popped out of my mouth before I could stop it: "What do you think about women wearing the *burqa* to cover their whole bodies or the *hijab* to cover their hair? My mother, sister, and sister-in-law wear the *hijab*, but if Muhammad were alive today, would he require that?"

He smiled, as if he'd heard this question many times before. "Let me ask you a question: Who understands a watch better—the person who created the watch or the person who buys the watch at a store and wears it?

"Its creator, naturally," I replied.

"In the same way, Allah understands the heart of man better than man himself. And Allah knows that it is better for all human beings if the woman covers herself so that she does not cause men to sin. Before Allah gave this revelation for women to cover up, the women of the Muslim community could be seen by all the men, so Allah blessed us with the revelation that women should be covered for the good of everyone. It is in the Quran for all to see and obey."

He certainly knows his Islamic theology, I thought. *Women today might not like what he has to say, but they couldn't argue with his logic.*

I enjoyed talking to Sheikh Ahmed. He was confident about what he believed but pleasant at the same time. I decided to ask Sheikh Ahmed about a comment he had made earlier. "Sheikh Ahmed, I've been thinking about what you said about the *hajj*. You said that it showed the world the power of the Muslim *ummah*. Why is it important to do that?"

"My son," he answered, "At the *hajj*, I see more than two million Muslims in one place, and I see that the people of Islam have the strength to make a change. The enemies of Islam destroyed the Islamic state and the physical power of Islam. But they weren't able to destroy the spiritual power of this religion or the Muslim people themselves. Allah will help the Muslim people to rise up again and restore that which was taken from them."

"Are you talking about restoring the caliphate?" I asked. "Some people say that Muhammad never wanted a caliph system. He didn't set one up before he died. In fact, he didn't give any instructions about what to do or who was to lead the Muslim nation after his death."

Sheikh Ahmed answered confidently, "Muhammad is the best example to follow. If he established an Islamic state with a central leader, then he established the pattern for the rest of history. He didn't need to give specific teaching about it. I can tell you for a fact that if the Prophet were alive today, he would never rest for one moment until the caliphate was restored. And after the Muslims were joined together in the caliphate, he would lead them in battle to bring the entire world into submission to the Islamic state."

I agreed with the goal of restoring the caliphate, but I was tired of the violence that Muslim groups were using to try to get it back. I said nothing for a moment.

Sheikh Ahmed turned to look at me intently. "My son, I spend a lot of time talking to people. I can tell when someone has a question that they haven't asked. I am here to talk to you. Why don't you say what is on your mind?"

I was a little worried. "You're not an undercover policeman, are you?" I said teasingly.

A little smile played across his face. "No, I'm not," he answered. "I'm just a slave of Allah, like you."

"Then I will be honest with you," I said. "When Hassan al-Banna started the Muslim Brotherhood in 1928, they set up schools, established mosques, and built factories. But then they started to use violence to overthrow the Egyptian government, and they assassinated the Egyptian prime minister in 1948. Since then many other Islamist groups have been formed. Many of them help the people by supporting schools or hospitals, but they also use violence and terrorism to try to establish Muslim governments. They are killing innocent people—a lot of them Muslims."

Sheikh Ahmed answered me confidently. "You must remember that these groups take action for the sake of the future of humanity. The leaders of the Islamic revival around the world do not kill just for the sake of killing, nor do they spread terrorism just for the cause of terrorizing people. No, they understand that their religion is in a direct confrontation with the system of man, and the system of man has to be eliminated so the system of Allah can be put in place all over the world."

Sheikh Ahmed's invitation to talk made me bold. I replied, "I agree with you that Allah's authority needs to be established throughout the entire world, but is it right for us to make this happen through violence? How can people believe Islam is a religion of peace when it is involved in almost every conflict in every part of the world?" After I asked the question, I realized I was on dangerous ground. I didn't want him to think I was questioning Islam.

To my relief, he stayed relaxed and responded to me with a gentle tone, like a teacher who was trying to explain an important idea to a struggling student.

"My son," he said, "yes, Islam is a religion of peace. Peace is one of the ninety-nine names of Allah. But you have to understand the meaning of peace from a Muslim point of view.

"First of all, the word *Islam* does not mean 'peace.' The word *Islam* means 'submission.' This is important because peace comes as a fruit of submission. For example, if two people are in conflict, and one submits to the other, then peace will be established. So you see, conflict may be necessary to bring the submission that brings peace. This is the destiny of Islam—to fight until submission and then peace is achieved."

I nodded as he spoke, while keeping my eyes on the highway. I was glad that the *hajj* traffic gave me an excuse not to look in his eyes. "Thank you," I said. "Your explanation is very clear." The Islamic understanding of peace was very different from the Western understanding, which sees peace as a "lack of conflict." The West wants to establish peace by tolerating differences, but Islam says peace only comes after the world fully accepts Islam. I wondered why Allah loved conflict so much.

The look on my face must have betrayed me. Sheikh Ahmed continued patiently, "My son, let us look at the life of the Prophet. As an Al-Azhar scholar, you know the Prophet received his first revelations from the angel Gabriel while he was living in Mecca. The people of Mecca viciously persecuted the Prophet for his teachings. He and his wife Khadija and his followers nearly starved to death in the desert because the people of his own tribe in Mecca would not sell them food. By the grace of Allah, the Meccans started to sell Muhammad food again, but they never stopped insulting him and threatening him.

"The Prophet didn't fight physically against the people of Mecca during that time because Allah had not yet given him weapons and an army. But the Prophet showed the Meccans their error with his preaching. And he warned them that he would not tolerate their abuse forever. He told them, 'O people of Mecca, I swear in the name of Allah I come as a slaughterer.' The Prophet finally rejected the people of Mecca and went to live with good people who accepted him in Medina and supplied him with an army and weapons. I ask you, what good did it do for Muhammad to tolerate the insults of the infidels of Mecca?"

I admitted, "Muhammad's tolerance did not change the attitude of the people of Mecca. They rejected his teaching anyway."

"That's why Allah gave Muhammad a new way," he continued. "After the Prophet emigrated to Medina, Allah told him, 'Permission is given to fight.' The Muslims do not need to allow themselves to be insulted or abused any longer. Then there was the glorious Battle of Badr! Allah gave the tiny Muslim army a surprise victory against an army from Mecca that was three times as large. That mighty victory showed all of Arabia that they could not abuse Islam and the Prophet any longer. Allah showed that he would fight alongside the Muslims until the whole world submitted to Islam.

"The glorious Quran says, 'And fight with them until there is no more persecution and religion should be only for Allah; but if they desist, then surely Allah sees what they do.'"

I saw one more chance to push for tolerance in the words of the Quran. "But the verse before that says, 'Say to those who have disbelieved, if they cease from disbelief, their past will be forgiven.'"

Sheikh Ahmed laughed, "That just means that when the unbelievers accept Islam, then they will be forgiven and Muslims can stop fighting them. If the unbelievers don't accept Islam, then Muslims will continue to fight them.

"The weak Muslims today want to go back to the Mecca days when Allah told us not to fight. Those days are over," he said firmly. "When Allah gave the Prophet soldiers and weapons in Medina, then Allah cancelled the old revelations about tolerance and replaced them with the new revelations of power. Islam is no longer weak. With our people and our oil resources, we have the power to fight and be the strongest empire on earth.

"The whole world can now be divided into two groups: *Dar-ul-Harb*, those in the House of War who refuse to accept Islamic law, and *Dar-ul-Islam*, those in the House of Peace."

Sheikh Ahmed had been gazing intently out the window as he spoke, as if he were looking for something. Suddenly he gestured to the right. "This is the place," he said confidently. "Pull over to the side of the road for a minute." I pulled over and looked at the right side of the road. All I saw was desert.

"What is it?" I asked.

"This is the place where Muhammad camped with his ten

thousand soldiers as he prepared to invade Mecca," he said with pride. "The Prophet divided his soldiers into four divisions, and each division attacked the city from a different direction. Allah showed the Prophet the strategy of attacking from four directions.

"Allah gave the Prophet a glorious victory that day. The people of Mecca were so terrified that they wouldn't even come out and fight. Allah made the Prophet more than a preacher. He was a victorious military leader. He accompanied the fighters on twenty-seven raids, and in nine of those raids he fought with them on the battlefield.

"Mustafa, Islam will achieve peace when the world submits to its authority. Does that make sense to you?"

"Yes, it does," I answered, but I felt conflict inside.

I drove in silence for a while, thinking about our conversation. I thought, *When I was doing the hajj, I was looking for a sign that Allah is pleased with me. Now here is a man full of faith in Allah who is willing to talk about the questions that have built up in my heart over the years. Maybe this is Allah's way of answering my prayer. I need to hear more of what he has to say.*

Chapter 7

The Mosque of the Prophet

Heat was shimmering on the highway as I reached the city of Medina, its skyline dominated by one thing—the massive Mosque of the Prophet with its ten graceful white minarets reaching toward the cloudless sky. No matter how many times you see it, the Mosque of the Prophet instills a feeling of awe, even with the flocks of hotels clustered around it like feeding birds. The complex can accommodate a half million people at one time. Muhammad built the original mosque the first year after he immigrated to Medina, but then it was barely more than a shack with palm trunks for pillars and a roof made out of palm fronds covered with mud.

I turned to look at Sheikh Ahmed as we approached the mosque. His eyes were sparkling, and he had a look of genuine pride and satisfaction on his face. "Whenever we see the mosque, I feel like I am home," he said. "Let's park, and I will show you around inside."

"I already have a hotel reservation," I said, "so we can park in their lot." I picked my way through the traffic to the gleaming white Moevenpick Hotel, with its unmistakable modern cube-shaped design. Established by a Swedish company, it was one of the finest hotels in the area. My father insisted on paying for me to stay there on my trip. He would have paid for me to stay in one of the finest hotels in Mecca too, but we couldn't get a reservation with short notice.

The Moevenpick Hotel was within eyesight of the famous Green Dome that marks Muhammad's tomb. It was a short walk to the entrance of the mosque, but I still had a hard time keeping up with Sheikh Ahmed. He walked briskly and leaned forward, as if he were climbing up a hill. *He sure does have a lot of energy for an older man, I thought again, hoping I would be able to keep up. Maybe it's all the coffee.*

The Mosque of the Prophet was congested with *hajj* pilgrims but not nearly as daunting as the crush of people circling al-Ka'aba. We washed and then walked barefoot on the polished stone floors through the arched doorways and white marble pillars. Inside was bright and airy, with richly embellished ceilings, towering pillars and arches, and polished brass embellishments everywhere.

The first thing we did was pray two *raka'ahs* of salutation and four *raka'ahs* for the noon prayer that we missed when we were in the car. A *raka'ah* [pronounced *RA-kah-ah*] is the standard unit of prayer that is used at every prayer time. Every prayer time requires a certain number of *raka'ahs*. For example, the dawn prayer is usually two raka'ahs. Whenever I made up for a prayer that I missed, I felt as if I were filling out a score card, but I didn't know how many points would make me the winner. As I knelt with my forehead touching the cool marble floor, I dutifully mentioned again all the requests that had been given to me by friends and family from home.

When we finished, Sheikh Ahmed reminded me, "Prayers in the Mosque of the Prophet are worth one thousand times more than prayers anywhere else."

I pointed to the other side of the mosque. "Let us show our respect to the Prophet now," and we blended into the river of pilgrims going in that direction. Our ears were filled with the steady murmur of pilgrims praying and greeting the Prophet. When we were close enough to see the ornate green and gold gate that protected the tomb, I spoke the traditional greeting: "May the peace, mercy, and blessing of Allah be upon you, O Prophet. May Allah grant you a good reward on behalf of your people." I didn't hear Sheikh Ahmed say anything, but I'm sure he must have.

Just a few steps to the right of Muhammad's tomb were the tombs of Abu Bakr and Umar ibn Al-Khattib, two of Muhammad's most loyal and important followers. I also spoke the greeting to them, and I heard Sheikh Ahmed saying the words too. After he was silent for a moment, I looked over at him, and he seemed deep in thought.

"What are you thinking about?" I asked.

"These were great men," he said. "I wish there were more men like them alive today. They knew how to fight for Islam. Umar was such a strong man; the Jewish people were all terrified of him. And Abu Bakr—the first mature man to accept Islam after Muhammad and the first caliph of the Muslim state. He stood by the Prophet all the way, defending him, and even giving him his daughter Aisha for a wife.

"Who is really loyal to the Prophet today? Who will defend him with their lives? That's the kind of Muslim you want to be, right, Mustafa?" he asked seriously. I was surprised by his question, but I nodded back at him quickly.

As we milled around with the other pilgrims, Sheikh Ahmed pulled me aside and guided me over to the other side of the room. "Speaking of Abu Bakr's daughter, look over there," he said, pointing to the back of the room. "The wives of the Prophet had their little houses right here along the outside wall of the mosque when it was first built. There was Aisha and Hafsa and Zaineb... The houses were so small that if you put your hand up, you would touch the ceiling. Aisha's house had a door that went into the mosque..." He paused. "The Prophet loved Aisha so much. And yet today so many Muslims have rejected her..." His voice trailed off. "She was a beautiful girl."

"She must have been," I murmured.

He continued, "Don't you remember how much the Prophet

loved her? He had a cup made of wood that he used for drinking water, honey, milk, or even wine—before Allah prohibited alcohol. Aisha liked to drink out of that cup too. After she drank, the Prophet would take the cup and drink from the same side that she used so that his mouth touched the place where her lips were on the cup."

"She was very young when they were married, wasn't she?"

"Yes," he said, "she was six years old when she became engaged to the Prophet, and she was nine years old when they were married and she went to live with him. She was a woman in a little girl's body. Remember when she got jealous of one of the Prophet's other wives? The Prophet had prepared a plate of food for a new wife, a beautiful Jewish teenager named Safiya. Aisha grabbed the plate of food and threw it on the floor, shattering the plate and scattering the food on the ground. She did this in front of their slaves. But Muhammad didn't reprimand her. He just said to the slaves, 'Aisha is jealous.'"

I was a little shocked. "I never heard that story before. How old was Aisha when she did this?"

"About ten or eleven. She had been Muhammad's wife for almost two years at this time."

I was amazed at how much detail Sheikh Ahmed knew about Muhammad's life with Aisha. He continued, "The Prophet stayed with a different wife every night of the week, but he spent almost all his days with Aisha. The angel Gabriel even had respect for Aisha. He came to the Prophet one time when he and Aisha were together in bed, and Gabriel turned his head away and made a noise so that the Prophet would know that Gabriel had come."

These memories seemed very vivid to Sheikh Ahmed. I decided that he was probably thinking about his own wife when he was describing Aisha. Sheikh Ahmed interrupted my thoughts. "The Prophet has so many memories here," he said. "Let's go out and greet his wives and companions in the al-Baqi Cemetery."

The al-Baqi Cemetery is the final resting place for more of Muhammad's wives and companions than any other place in the world. Some say that nearly seven thousand companions of the Prophet are buried there. As we walked out of the mosque and through the al-Baqi Gate, I noticed a sign that read, "No Women Permitted." *That's interesting*, I thought to myself. *There are a few women in the cemetery already, including the Prophet's wives. I guess you can't keep them all out!*

As soon as we stepped out of the mosque, the afternoon sun almost blinded us. Before us lay fourteen acres of flat, bleached-out sand, crisscrossed by a handful of wide cement walkways. The land was almost completely barren—no trees, no grave markers, just a few stones to mark the boundary between the original, smaller cemetery and the expansion. Al-Baqi literally means "garden of trees," but there was not even a blade of grass living in this barren landscape. My companion growled, "I would show my respect for the companions of the Prophet and his wives more than this," he said. "When the Prophet buried his first companion, he even had to cut down trees to make a space for him—this was such a lush, beautiful place. Allah will pay the people for the disrespect they have shown here."

The graves were not marked, but Sheikh Ahmed seemed to know exactly where to find certain ones. He took pleasure in describing them to me. "Here," he said pointing to the left, "is the grave of one of the Prophet's aunts. She was a kind woman." He turned toward the patch of sand and spoke the traditional greeting over her grave: "May the peace, mercy, and blessing of Allah be upon you. May Allah be pleased with you and grant you a good reward on behalf of Muhammad's people."

Just a little further down the path, Sheikh Ahmed stopped and then gestured toward another area of sand. I saw that his eyes were glistening as he spoke. "And here is the grave of the Prophet's son Ibrahim—only ten months old when he died. The Prophet never had a son who grew up to be a man. He is in Allah's hands now." He spoke the greeting over Ibrahim's grave as well.

"There are so many of the Prophet's family here. Almost all his wives are buried in this cemetery. Here is Aisha's site. And not far from it are Hafza, Juwayriya, Sawda, Zaynab Bint Khuzaima, Zaynab bint Jahsh, Umm Habiba, and Umm Salama. And the grave of his pretty Jewish wife, Safiya bint Ho-yay, is here too. She was a teenager when she became one of the Prophet's wives." He paused at Safiya's grave. "Aisha was always jealous of Safiya. She probably doesn't like being buried so close to her," he said smiling. For each wife's grave, he paused and spoke the greeting.

It took a long time for him to greet so many of the Prophet's wives. After all, Muhammad married a total of thirteen women during the course of his life, and almost all of them were buried in this cemetery. The Quran allows Muslim men to have up to four wives at a time, but it says that Muhammad could marry as many wives as he wanted (Surah 33:50).

Then Sheikh Ahmed turned to look toward the right side of the gate. "This is the part of al-Baqi that makes my blood boil with anger," he said. "It is the grave of one of the Prophet's beloved grandsons, Hassan ibn Ali. He was poisoned by an evil traitor of the Prophet's family named Muawiyya."

"I know what you mean, Sheikh Ahmed," I agreed. "I studied Muawiyya and his family for my master's thesis. Muawiyya even walked with Muhammad and wrote down parts of the Quran. He was there to see Muhammad play with his grandsons, and yet he still poisoned one of them—Hassan ibn Ali. And before Muawiyya died, he commanded his son Yazid to murder Muhammad's other grandson, Husayn ibn Ali. So he destroyed the Prophet's family."

"As Allah is my witness," Sheikh Ahmed said, "that man is being tortured in his grave like no other before him because of what he did."

Sheikh Ahmed turned to the grave, "O Ali, may the peace, mercy, and blessing of Allah be upon you. But may the curses of Allah rain upon Muawiyya and his family forever."

It felt good to hear Sheikh Ahmed speak out against Muawiyya.

When I researched his life for my master's thesis, I remember how furious I felt. It is Muawiyya's fault that the Muslim people are divided into two camps—Sunni and Shia. Muwaiyya had blocked Muhammad's son-in-law, Ali ibn Abu Talib, from taking complete leadership of the Muslim state after the third caliph was assassinated. So instead of uniting under one leader, the Muslims were divided. Those who followed Ali became the Shia sect, and those who followed Muawiyya became the Sunni sect. They have been at war ever since.

Sheikh Ahmed stared grimly at the sand and then said to me. "Do you realize that Hassan's mother Fatima is buried just a few yards away from her murdered son's grave? She was the Prophet's favorite daughter, and when the Prophet died, she grieved so deeply that she died just a few months later. O daughter Fatima, how your heart has been broken! May the peace, mercy, and blessing of Allah be upon you."

After several minutes, he gazed across the cemetery and began walking briskly toward a newer section. He talked as he walked.

"Even the Prophet's father is buried in this cemetery now. You know, the Prophet never met his father. While the Prophet's mother was pregnant, his father went on a caravan trip. On his way back to Mecca, he became ill and stopped in a village named Banu Najar to try to get help, but suddenly he died, and they buried him there. He was only twenty-five years old. His gravesite has been moved several times, and now it is here."

We walked a little further. "And here is one more special lady—Halima As-Sadyah. Do you know the Prophet lived with her and her Bedouin tribe for the first four years of his life? She nursed him, so she is his mother in nursing according to Islamic law. Do you know what a mother in nursing is?"

"Of course I do," I answered, surprised by the question. Under Islamic law, when a woman nurses a child, she becomes that child's mother in nursing. I felt very uncomfortable with Sheikh Ahmed's question, but I reassured myself that there was no way Sheikh Ahmed could know that my mother in nursing was a Christian.

"A mother in nursing has a powerful influence on a child," said Sheikh Ahmed. "The Prophet had a close bond with his mother in nursing. She even accepted Islam later in life, and that is how she came to be buried in this cemetery."

Why is he talking so much about the Prophet's mother in nursing? I wondered. *Is there any way he could know about the Christian woman who nursed me?* All I wanted to do was change the subject. I noticed how he seemed relatively comfortable despite the sun beating down on our heads.

"Sheikh Ahmed," I said, "I am jealous of your turban. It seems to keep you cooler than I am."

"You should try it," he said. "The Prophet recommended it for all his followers."

I continued to trail after him as he raced through acres of sand, pointing out other gravesites—cousins, uncles, and other companions of the Prophet. Important Muslims from later centuries were buried there as well. He would pause and greet almost everyone, both men and women.

Finally he said, "I've seen almost everyone in Medina except one very dear to the Prophet." He continued, "I'd like to see the grave of the Prophet's mother. Can you drive me there?"

"Of course," I answered. "It would be my honor."

A Mysterious Phone Call

It was a short drive from Medina to al-Abwa, a tiny undeveloped village about fourteen miles (23 kilometers) from Medina, where the grave of Muhammad's mother was located.

As we bumped over the crumbling two-lane road, Sheikh Ahmed asked me, "Tell me more about your mother."

I answered, "She is one of the sweetest, most loving ladies you will ever meet. She especially likes serving guests who come to our house. When she was young, she was considered one of the most beautiful girls in our entire region."

"The Prophet's mother was also known for her beauty and kindness," he said. "And his father was known as one of the bravest young men in Mecca. Every girl in Mecca wanted to be engaged to him.

"Did you know the Prophet's mother died because she wanted her little boy to see his father's grave? When Muhammad was six years old, his mother took him to the village where Muhammad's father died before Muhammad was even born. They saw his father's grave, but on the way back home, his mother started complaining that she had a fever. Little Muhammad tried to help her. He wiped her face with water and gave a drink.

"They continued to try to reach Mecca, but she got weaker and weaker until they reached the place where we are going now—al-Abwa—and she could walk no further. There they sat on the sand—Muhammad, his mother, and their maidservant. The servant massaged his mother's head, face, arms, and chest to try to help her, but it was the time for her to depart, and she died. Muhammad went into shock, running in circles around her body, weeping, as the servant tried to console him. People from the area came and buried Muhammad's mother there where she died. So the Prophet became an orphan at the age of six.

"Remember what the Prophet said: Paradise is under the feet of your mother," he finished. "Not everyone has the joy of being with their mother on this earth. Pray for her while you can."

My companion sighed when we arrived at the site. There was nothing more than a raised bed of sand. Pilgrims had gathered chunky rocks about the size of soccer balls and placed them in a thick ring around the grave. A few women were gathered at the site, quietly praying.

"She died before Islam," Sheikh Ahmed said simply. "The Prophet asked Allah permission to beg forgiveness for her, but Allah did not grant it. Then the Prophet asked permission to visit the grave and Allah agreed." He stepped away from me to stand near the raised bed of earth alone.

After a long time, he walked back to me. "It is good to visit graves because they make you mindful of death," he said. "Serve Allah while you can because after you die, you will face the results of your choice. Did Allah choose to give her a little Paradise in her grave as she awaits Judgment Day? Or is she being burned and tortured during this time because she never accepted Islam? Only Allah knows."

I thought of my own mother and how I would feel when she was in the grave. *At least she is a good Muslim,* I reasoned. *She has worked hard for Allah's mercy.* But I knew that Islam does not guarantee that the pious will be comforted in the grave. That decision would be made by Allah alone. He will consider the good works, but we can never know how he will judge them. The only sure way to reach Paradise is to die while fighting in jihad.

Why couldn't Allah give Muhammad more revelations about the future of our souls? We Muslims live in a state of unresolved terror. No matter how hard we try, there is no peace of mind about our lives after death. For the longest time, I wanted to talk with someone about that question, but I never had the courage. It might sound too critical of Islam. I thought about bringing it up with Sheikh Ahmed, but I decided that I would have to know him better before I approached a subject like that.

As we neared the hotel, Sheikh Ahmed said, "I have enjoyed our time and conversation together, Mustafa the Egyptian. It seems like there is so much more we could talk about. But I need to go to Egypt to meet with some friends, so I am afraid that we will have to part ways."

How interesting that he needs to go to Egypt, I thought. *Perhaps I can invite him to visit my family.*

I cleared my throat. "I'm going to spend the night in Medina and then drive to Jedda to fly back home to Cairo," I explained. "I think my family would enjoy meeting you. Would you be my guest at my father's house for a few days before you meet your friends? I could also show you around the Al-Azhar campus."

"By Allah," he said, "that is an excellent idea. I accept your invitation with gladness."

"This is excellent," I said. "I'm only sorry that I didn't ask you when we were in Mecca so that you could pack for the trip."

"It's no problem," he answered, smiling a little. "These are my favorite clothes. And I have everything else I need in my bag." He held up the rough brown bag that was always slung over his shoulder.

"You are welcome to stay in my hotel room with me," I said. "But I will also try to get you a room for yourself so that you can have your privacy."

"As you like," he answered.

When we reached the Moevenpick Hotel where I had my reservation, I asked Sheikh Ahmed to have a seat in the lobby while I tried to get a room for him. In reality, I didn't have much hope with all the pilgrims in town. "I don't think I have any empty rooms," the desk clerk said as he tapped the computer keyboard. Then he paused. "Wait," he said. "There has just been a cancellation for a room right next to you."

"That's perfect; I'll take it," I answered. I pulled out a credit card from my father to pay for the rooms. My father was well-known for his hospitality and generosity, so I knew he wouldn't mind paying for my guest.

"Mustafa," my companion asked as I rejoined him in the lobby, "were you able to get an extra room?"

"Yes," I replied.

"Allah be praised," he answered. "Now quickly—let's get some coffee before we go to the sunset prayer. I see a café over there." We only had a few minutes, so we took our coffee in paper cups and headed out to the street to walk to the mosque.

We weren't the only ones with coffee cups in hand on the way to the Mosque of the Prophet. Most pilgrims were running on coffee and adrenaline. For many, this was the only trip to the land of the Prophet they would take in their lifetimes, and they didn't want to waste a single minute.

Rather than being frustrated by the crowds, Sheikh Ahmed seemed to be energized by them. As we looked for a place to pray in the lines, he said with satisfaction, "May the Prophet's mosque be this full of life every day."

By the time we returned to the hotel, I was eager for a good rest in a comfortable bed. I wished him a good night, and we went to our separate rooms. My cell phone battery was dead, so I picked up the hotel phone to make a quick call home to let them know I was doing well. My mother answered.

"O my son, I am so happy to hear the sound of your voice. Are you well? Was your *hajj* successful?"

"Yes, Mother," I answered. "This has been an incredible trip. I've met a very interesting man in Mecca who has a deep understanding of Islam and the life of Muhammad. I've invited him to spend a few days at our home in Cairo."

"Your father and I will be looking forward to the honor of his visit," she said happily. "We will make him most comfortable."

"I know you will, Mother. I know you will."

"Don't worry about getting a taxi when you arrive at the airport," she said. "Your father will pick you up."

As we talked, I pushed the curtains away from the sliding glass doors and looked at the amazing view of the mosque, with the green dome over the Prophet's tomb in front of me. I slid open the door and stepped out onto the balcony. To my surprise, I heard the voice of Sheikh Ahmed in the other room. He was talking earnestly to someone, but I was astonished to hear that he was not speaking Arabic. He was having a conversation in an Asian language that I did not recognize. *This man is not as simple as he seems to be, I thought. I wonder who he is talking to.*

I awoke the next morning at 4:30 to the sound of knocking on my door. "I'm coming," I called out, hurrying to the door and opening it.

"Peace be upon you," said Sheikh Ahmed. His beard and face were shining again, and the scent of sandalwood was in the air. "We need to be awake in plenty of time for the dawn prayer. I'm going to the café to get some coffee, and I'll meet you there."

"Yes," I mumbled, "thank you," wondering where he got his energy. When I got to the lobby, I stopped at the front desk for just a moment. "Out of curiosity," I said, "do I have any phone charges to my rooms from last night?"

"Yes," he replied. "There is one call from your room."

"What about my friend's room?" I asked.

"The phone wasn't used at all," he replied.

[Chapter 9]

Suicide Shame

Sheikh Ahmed handed me a cup of coffee as we walked to the Mosque of the Prophet for dawn prayers. When we finished, we went back to the hotel café for breakfast.

Sheikh Ahmed didn't look at the menu, but he asked the server, "Can you do a special order for me?"

"We will do our best," she replied pleasantly.

"I'd like plain yogurt with honey and a dish of dates on the side. Can you do that?"

"Yes, sir," she answered. "It will be our pleasure."

Sheikh Ahmed was pleased. "This is a nice place, even if it is run by non-Muslims," he said. "So, what are the plans for today?"

"Well," I answered, "I think we should drive to Jeddah as soon as possible and get to the airport. It may be difficult to get a plane ticket for you."

He reassured me, "I don't think it will be a problem, but I look forward to seeing your family, so I am glad to leave early."

"By the way," I said, "last night I heard you talking on the phone, and I wanted to let you know that I will be happy to pay any phone expense you might have."

"Don't worry about it," he replied. "I have my own phone."

I thought to myself, *I didn't think Sheikh Ahmed would be the type to carry around a cell phone.*

"Could I ask you one more question?" I said.

"Sure," he replied.

"What language were you speaking last night?"

"Oh," he said. "I believe that was Malay. Or you might have heard English."

"How did you learn to speak those languages?" I asked in amazement.

Sheikh Ahmed replied, "Allah has helped me to learn many languages because I have friends all over the world. Sometimes they have questions, so I talk with them on my cell phone. Allah wants his people to take advantage of all the advances in technology. In the seventh century, the Prophet communicated through letters sealed with his silver ring. But if the Prophet were alive today, you can be sure he would be using all the modern communication technologies, including the internet and television."

Ironically, the hotel had a television in the corner of the café, and we watched it as we ate our dates and yogurt. The television was tuned to a famous Middle East news station where the news announcer was telling about a suicide bomber attack at a police station in Iraq. "Sheikh Ahmed," I asked, "what do you think of suicide bombers?"

"First of all, I would say that I am very proud of them," he replied without hesitation. "These people are using the most powerful weapon they have—their bodies. That weapon is given to them by Allah himself. The enemy cannot stop that kind of weapon because it is out of his power. These suicide bombers are heroes and died as martyrs, and they are in Paradise today. Allah guarantees that the person who dies while fighting jihad will enter into Paradise. As it says in *Surah Al-Qital*, 'Whoso fights in the cause of Allah, and is killed or gets victory, we shall bestow on him a great reward' (Surah 47:4). And also, 'Think not of those who are killed in the Way of Allah as dead. Nay, they are alive, with their Lord, and they have provision' (Surah 3:169–171, Muhsin Khan)."

I couldn't believe my ears. I asked, "But isn't suicide prohibited in the Quran? Surah Al-Baqarah says, 'Make not your own hands contribute to your destruction' (Surah 2:195), and *Surah an-Nisai* says, 'Nor kill (or destroy) yourselves' (Surah 4:29).

"Even the Prophet said, 'Whoever throws himself down from a mountain and kills himself, he will be in the fire of hell throwing himself down for ever and ever. Whoever drinks poison and kills himself will have the poison in his hand, drinking it in the fire of hell for ever and ever. Whoever kills himself with a piece of iron, or a weapon, will have that piece of iron in his hand, stabbing himself in the stomach with it in the fire of hell forever and ever.'"

Sheikh Ahmed quickly put down my argument. "My son," he said, "these verses are about someone intentionally killing themselves for selfish reasons that will not benefit Islam. A suicide bomber is giving his or her life to Allah strategically with a goal in mind. There is a story about a poor man who was standing nearby as the Prophet was sending his soldiers off to battle. This man heard Muhammad say, 'Paradise is under the shadow of the sword.' He said good-bye to his friends, took the sheath off his sword and broke it, and then ran into the battle. He knew that he would not come back alive. He fought until he was killed because he knew that he would enter Paradise."

I was incredulous. "So are you saying that suicide bombing is a good thing?"

"No," he replied. "It is not a good thing. It is a shame that faithful Muslim people are forced into this position. Suicide bombings are only needed because the Islamic caliphate was destroyed in 1924. When Islam once again has its own state and own military, then the Islamic military will deal with the enemies of Islam, and there will not be a need for suicide operations."

I risked asking one more question. "In this attack at the police station, there was a woman and child who were killed on the street outside the station. Suicide bombers kill many people who are not involved in fighting. Doesn't Islam prohibit this?"

Sheikh Ahmed answered, "This is a problem in any kind of war, and the hadith says the Prophet disapproved of killing women and children. But there are exceptions. One day a man asked the Prophet, 'Is it permissible to attack pagan warriors at night when their women and children would probably be exposed to danger?' The Prophet said, 'Yes, I consider the women and children as of their parents.' So women and children who are mixed in with the enemy may be killed as part of fighting the enemy. "

I thought to myself, *Is this really what Allah meant for his people—that they would cause terror throughout the world and even kill women and children?*

After breakfast, we went back to our rooms to get our things. My friend didn't need much time to pack—he just came out of the room with his rough cloth sack slung over his shoulder.

The Jeddah-Medinah Road took us quickly out of Medina, and we began the four-hour drive to the airport.

"I hope we will be able to get a ticket for you to Cairo," I said. "It's going to be really crowded."

"Allah will help us," Sheikh Ahmed replied. "Don't worry about it."

"Tell me," he said, "what are your plans while you are at Al-Azhar?"

"I just finished my PhD in Islamic history and culture," I answered. "Now I have the honor of lecturing full-time to the students studying for their bachelor's degrees."

"Al-Azhar has served Islam for more than a thousand years. It is the heart and brain of the Islamic world, is it not?"

"Yes, it is."

"Then you are a spiritual leader in the Muslim

world—correct?"

"Yes," I answered, starting to wonder where he was heading with his questions.

"Mustafa, what kind of leader do you want to be?"

His question caught me completely off guard. I felt my throat tightening, and my mind raced for an acceptable answer.

"Where are you going to lead the students who come to your classes? What are you going to teach them?"

Finally, my mind cleared enough for me to speak. "I will teach them according to the example of the Apostle of Allah," I said, my heart pounding. "Being a Muslim means to worship Allah and to follow the example of his Prophet."

"You have answered well," he said. "I see that desire in you. But I also see the hesitation. Where does the hesitation come from?"

My heart was still pounding. *Does he know what I've been thinking? Does he know my doubts? Was my soul ruined by the Christian lady who nursed me?*

"I only hesitate because of the greatness of the task before me," I stammered.

"Allah will help you," he said firmly. "Allah helps the man who leads others on the straight path."

There was an awkward moment of silence before I finally spoke. "You are right, Sheikh Ahmed. There is hesitation in my voice. Sometimes I am not sure which path the Prophet would take. I only wish that I could see him and speak to him myself. Then I would be sure that I am doing the right thing."

"My son," he said, "the Prophet gave you something to hold on to that will bring you life. It is the Quran (Surah 7:170). You know the words of the Quran by heart. And the Prophet left his example. This is something you have studied for years. If you just look at what you already have in front of you, you will know exactly what the Prophet would say or do."

I answered, "You are right, Sheikh Ahmed. The Quran is the

lamp of my life. I just wonder if the Prophet would act differently in modern society than he did in the seventh century. Did the Prophet intend for the Muslim world to continue living as he lived fourteen hundred years ago?"

"The Prophet knows more about the modern world than you may think," said Sheikh Ahmed.

Enemies of Islam

I continued to drive toward the Jeddah airport, thinking about what Sheikh Ahmed had said. I felt uncomfortable that he sensed my doubt, but he also seemed very patient with me. *If he is willing to answer questions, then I might as well ask them, I thought. The only problem is that I might not like the answer.*

Aloud I said, "Sheikh Ahmed, what do you think the Prophet would say about 9/11? Would he agree with attacking the United States?"

"Let me ask you a question," he answered. "Was the United States a friend of Islam or an enemy of Islam?"

"I would say a little bit of both," I answered. "The United States supports secular Muslim governments who in turn persecute those who want to bring Islamic law back to society. But at the same time the United States rescued the Muslims of Kuwait from Saddam Hussein and the Muslims of Bosnia from genocide."

Sheikh Ahmed was quick to dismiss any good America might have done. "Don't be deceived when America seems to rescue Muslims from danger," he corrected me sharply. "America is only looking after her own interests. Her goal is still to destroy Islam through supporting secular governments in the Muslim world."

Sheikh Ahmed continued, "You need to look at how the Prophet dealt with his own America—the city of Mecca. In the seventh century, Mecca was the capital of evil. Today I say America is the capital of all evil.

"In the seventh century, the Prophet defeated Mecca and sent a declaration to all Arabia saying that Islam would conquer them too. On 9/11 the hijackers dealt a severe blow to America and sent a message to the whole world that Islam has a long arm that can reach anywhere.

"In the seventh century, Mecca was the first city to declare war on the Muslims. Today America declared war against Islam three ways. First, she took the side of Israel to establish the Jewish state on the holy land of Muslims. Second, she propped up secular, infidel governments in Islamic countries. And third, she invaded the independent Muslim countries of Afghanistan and Iraq and declared a worldwide war against the most faithful Muslims—the war on terrorism. These three acts are all the justification the Muslim world needs to fight back. The Quran tells you, "To those against whom war is made, permission is given to fight because they are wronged;—and verily Allah is most powerful for their aid (Surah 22:39)."

Sheikh Ahmed concluded, "Do you see, Mustafa the Egyptian, how America is the enemy of Islam?"

How could I argue against his logic? I would look as if I were betraying my own faith.

Sheikh Ahmed had more to say. "So, if America is the enemy of Islam, then we must deal with America the way the Prophet dealt with his enemies. Do you remember what happened at the Battle of the Trench?"

I knew the story well and answered, "Yes, the Muslims dug a trench around the city of Medina for protection, and then the people of Mecca and the Jews of Qurayza put the city under siege for nearly a month. There was little fighting except for some exchange of arrows and a fight between Ali and one of the Meccans. During the siege, three Meccans were killed, one Jew, and one Muslim."

"Do you know how the siege ended?" said Sheikh Ahmed. "It

is one of my favorite stories."

"Yes," I answered, not surprised that Sheikh Ahmed liked this story. "During the siege, a man named Nu'aym converted to Islam secretly and came to Muhammad. He was from the Ghatafan tribe, which was allied with the Meccans. He told Muhammad, 'My own people do not know that I have converted.' Muhammad replied, 'Go back to your people and awaken distrust among them so that they will give up this siege against us. Remember: war is deceit.'"

Sheikh Ahmed nodded with satisfaction and then finished the story for me. "Nu'aym played his part brilliantly. He told the Jewish tribe, 'Don't help the Meccans and the Ghatafan tribe fight Muhammad unless you get some of their people to hold as hostages. Otherwise they may pull back while you are fighting and leave you to fight Muhammad alone.' Then Nu'aym went to the people of Mecca and the Ghatafan tribe and said, 'The Jews have secretly converted to Islam. They are going to ask you for some people to hold as hostages, but they actually promised Muhammad that they would bring him some of your people so Muhammad could cut off their heads.'"

Sheikh Ahmed smiled broadly. "The scheme worked perfectly. The Ghatafan tribe sent a message to the Jews saying that they needed help to fight Muhammad. The Jews from Qurayzah asked for hostages, and the Ghatafan tribe refused. The same thing happened between the Jews and the people of Mecca, so the whole alliance was destroyed, thanks be to Allah. They ended the siege, and the Prophet and his people were spared." Sheikh Ahmed concluded with obvious delight.

"Now, back to the topic we were discussing," he said seriously. "I've already told you that America is an enemy of Islam, especially because she supports the state of Israel. So to deal with this situation, we need to see how the Prophet responded to his enemies, especially the Jews. What did he do to the Jews of Qurayzah who plotted against him? Did he give them another chance to attack him?"

"No," I answered. "The angel Gabriel told Muhammad to attack the people of Qurayzah. Muhammad and his army went to the village, which was about five miles from Mecca, and held it under siege for twenty-five days. During the siege Muhammad brought his soldiers close to the edge of the city and shouted at the people, 'O children of the monkeys and the pigs, I have come to slaughter you.' After the surrender, Muhammad's military took all the men, tied their hands behind their backs, and forced them to march the five miles back to the center of Medina. Muslims stood all along the sides of the road and made fun of them."

"You are correct," said Sheikh Ahmed. "You know your history well. Then what did Muhammad do with these prisoners?"

I felt sick to my stomach as I visualized the rest of the story in my mind. It felt as if I were there, seeing the horror on the faces of the Jewish women and children as Muhammad took vengeance on the village. Sheikh Ahmed waited for me until I continued. "When the prisoners arrived in Medina, Muhammad commanded some of his soldiers to dig a large trench. Then he made the seven hundred Jewish men from the village stand in two lines facing the trench. The soldiers got a piece of wood and laid it on the ground at the edge of the trench. The two Jews at the front of the line had to lie on the ground with their necks on top of the piece of wood. Then two Muslim soldiers lifted up their swords and beheaded them. The Muslim soldiers threw their bodies in the pit and then dragged the next two men forward. The women and children were forced to watch."

I shuddered as I saw the picture in my mind. Muhammad had lost one Muslim in the Battle of the Trench; he responded by slaughtering seven hundred men. The Jewish wives and children must have been hysterical with grief and terror. When a Muslim soldier tried to drag the rabbi of the village to the trench, the rabbi fought with him desperately, and the soldier hit him in the face so hard that blood ran out of the rabbi's nose. The soldier said, "I see you want to save your life. You can save it with one word; just accept Islam." The rabbi answered defiantly, "I will never say those words because I do not believe in Islam or Muhammad. Even if you cut off my head a thousand times, I will never say it."

I was lost in this scene until I heard Sheikh Ahmed exclaim triumphantly, "You see! The Prophet dealt with his enemies aggressively because he had to defend the religion. When the Prophet lived in Mecca, he answered his enemies softly because Allah had not yet given him the ability to defend his religion. But after Muhammad moved to Medina, Allah gave him permission to fight his enemies. The new revelation of fighting cancelled out the older revelation of tolerance. This is a basic principle of understanding the Quran: the new cancels out the old.

"Islam is not a religion of weakness. It is a religion of strength. Do you think that Allah has changed his mind in the twenty-first century? Do you think Allah wants Muslims to submit to their enemies now?"

"No," I said, trying to sound enthusiastic. "You are right." In reality, my heart sank at his words. This was exactly the logic that was crippling my faith. Islam established a pattern of bloodshed in the seventh century that continued to the present day. Why couldn't Muslims put other religions in the "House of Peaceful Co-existence" instead of the "House of War"? Sometimes I just wanted to stand up and shout, "Why does Allah need us to fight for him? Why doesn't he defend his religion himself? The God of the Quran seems more interested in killing and conquering than in anything else." But these thoughts were too dangerous to express to anyone in the Muslim community, including a devout old man in a robe and turban.

Sheikh Ahmed looked at me. "Did you know that the Quran gave the heroes of 9/11 the strategy they used in the glorious attack against America?" he asked.

"No, I didn't," I said with some anxiety. I was not a fan of America's foreign policy, but I didn't think it was right for the hijackers to kill so many civilians. My opinion was definitely in the minority.

"Yes," he answered. "Go to *Surah Al-Hashr* [The Gathering]. It's talking about the People of the Book, specifically the Jews, and how Allah helped the Prophet to defeat them. I guarantee the hijackers were thinking of that passage when they came up with their plan.

"I know that verse," I said, and I quoted it in Arabic:

> It is He Who got out the Unbelievers among the People of the Book from their homes at the first gathering (of the forces). Little did ye think that they would get out: And they thought that their fortresses would defend them from Allah! But the (Wrath of) Allah came to them from quarters from which they little expected (it), and cast terror into their hearts, so that they destroyed their dwellings by their own hands and the hands of the Believers; take warning, then, O ye with eyes (to see)! (Surah 59:2).

"Mustafa," said Sheikh Ahmed, "let me tell you how the 9/11 attacks match this verse exactly.

"First, the Quran says 'they thought that their fortresses would defend them from Allah.' America thought the Atlantic Ocean would protect her."

"Second, the Quran says they 'destroyed their dwellings by their own hands and the hands of the Believers.' Do you see how the hijackers destroyed the American 'dwellings' using Americans' own hands—their own airplanes?

"Third, the Quran says the 'wrath of Allah came to them from quarters from which they little expected (it) and cast terror into their hearts.' America had no idea that her own airplanes could become weapons to be used against her. The people were paralyzed with terror; for days no airplanes flew in the skies."

Sheikh Ahmed had a look of satisfaction on his face. He paused to let his words sink in. But I felt a growing disappointment. I thought, *If Muslims literally follow the example of the Prophet, then they will attack any group that they see as an enemy. Muslims will forever be in conflict with the rest of the world. They will fight jihad until Judgment Day.*

Sheikh Ahmed was determined to prove his point. "Mustafa," Sheikh Ahmed said, "you know the Quran says the angels of Allah strike terror in the hearts of the unbelievers. That is exactly what happened on 9/11. The Quran says, 'Remember thy Lord inspired the angels (with the message): "I am with you: give firmness to the Believers: I will instill terror into the hearts of the Unbelievers: smite ye above their necks and smite all their finger-tips off them"' (Surah 8:12–13)."

Sheikh Ahmed finally noticed my silence. I knew I had to say something. "Allah be praised," I murmured, trying to look excited about what Sheikh Ahmed had said. "May it be so to all the enemies of Islam."

He nodded and smiled with satisfaction, as if he had accomplished an important goal.

Inside I was fighting a battle between reality and "want-to-be." *Mustafa*, I told myself, *you may need to learn to live with disappointment. The reality of Islam may not be the way you want it to be. This man isn't inventing Islamic history. He's just applying it to modern life. Keep an open mind. If Allah sent him to you, then he must be telling the truth.*

[Chapter 11]

The Afghani Man

The four-hour drive passed quickly, and by mid afternoon we arrived at the King Abdul Aziz International Airport just outside of Jeddah City. The airport was crowded and chaotic—typical for the *hajj* season. Even though I was uncomfortable with our conversation about 9/11 in the car, I still looked forward to introducing Sheikh Ahmed to my family. "Please have a seat while I find out about an airplane ticket for you," I said to Sheikh Ahmed. "There is no reason for us both to stand."

"Thank you," he said. "Your hospitality is most gracious."

I joined the long line for the EgyptAir ticket agent. I tried to be optimistic, but finding an empty seat on a plane to Cairo looked impossible. When I reached the ticket agent, he looked whipped.

"Hello," I said. "I have a ticket for the flight to Cairo at 5:00 p.m. I have a friend who would like to fly with me. Are there any seats available on that flight?"

"I'm surprised you are even asking that question," he replied irritably. "Don't you see all these people? But I'll check."

A few moments later he said, "That's interesting. Two seats in first class just opened up. Someone must have cancelled. I can give you those seats if you can pay for them right now."

I quickly pulled out my credit card and waved to Sheikh Ahmed to come to the ticket counter.

"When do we leave?" he asked.

"Five o'clock," I answered. "First class."

"Excellent," he nodded. He handed the ticket agent a few documents and said, "Do you mind filling out the forms for me?" I cringed as I waited for the ticket agent's response. "No problem," he answered without even looking up from the computer. Within a few minutes, he handed us boarding passes.

This was truly a miracle, as unbelievable as splitting the moon in half. "I need to travel with you all the time," I joked.

"As you like," he said. "But there is one condition."

"Yes, I know. You need coffee. Let's find some before we need to catch the bus to board the plane."

To get to our plane we had to go to the *hajj* terminal, which can hold up to eighty thousand people and is estimated to be the fourth largest terminal in the world. I wondered if Shiekh Ahmed had been flying since the airlines started more security checks after 9/11.

As we stood in the line to have our bags X-rayed and to walk through the metal detector, I asked, "What do you think of all this extra security? Is it fair?"

He frowned as an airline worker motioned for him to put his bag through the X-ray machine. After gazing at the computer monitor for a long time, the screener finally said, "You certainly have a lot of..."

"I know," he interrupted. "I'll take my bag now, thank you."

I wanted to ask Sheikh Ahmed what was in his bag, but I could see that question would not be welcomed.

The bus ride out to the plane was a hot, sweaty experience. When we finally settled into our seats for the two-hour flight to Cairo, the attendant offered us some magazines. I wanted to catch up on the news, so I took a few. Sheikh Ahmed did not take a magazine, but he said, "You can tell me what's new."

I flipped through a news magazine and noticed a picture of an Afghan man with the headline: "Afghan Christian convert could be executed."

"Who is that?" Sheikh Ahmed asked, looking at the picture.

I answered, "This man is making headlines around the world. He is an Afghani who converted to Christianity in 1990 and left his country. He returned to Afghanistan recently and was arrested and is on trial for rejecting Islam. What do you think of that?"

Sheikh Ahmed replied, "I thank Allah that the government of Afghanistan is standing up for Islam. The judgment of apostasy was set up by Allah to protect Islam and to stop a rebellious person from harming the faith. That is why the Prophet said, 'Anyone who changes his religion, kill him.' All the scholars agree that this saying is accurate, and you can see the Muslim community acting on it as well.

"These Western countries who are putting pressure on Afghanistan are hypocrites. They have laws against treason in their countries. This is the same situation. When a person leaves Islam, he has betrayed his religion, and there is a punishment for that."

I decided to challenge him a little. "The Western countries allow people to freely change religions. They say it is a basic human right. Even some Islamic scholars say that apostates should be left alone because the Quran does not say specifically that they must be killed. They say Allah punishes the apostates after they die."

Sheikh Ahmed replied sharply, "Those weak scholars have weak hearts and do not understand one of the most basic principles in Islamic law: if there is something not mentioned in the Quran, Allah made the hadith available. And if something is explained clearly in the hadith, then Muslims are required to accept that judgment. If a judgment is not mentioned by word in the Quran but it is mentioned in the hadith, Muslims have to practice it from the hadith.

"The Prophet said, 'The blood of a Muslim cannot be shed except in three cases—punishment for murder, punishment for adultery, and leaving Islam.'"

I looked again at the picture on the page. *All he wanted to do was have the freedom to think and to choose,* I thought. *It seems as if we Muslims are the people with the least freedom of all.*

I thought about one time when I was walking home from high school and saw a crowd gathered at a train track. A man had been pushed onto the track in front of a speeding train and killed. I thought maybe he had committed adultery or had an argument with someone, but then the people told me, "He became an apostate and his relatives threw him in front of the train to kill him." I also heard of several apostates who were poisoned by their families. I only heard of one time when an apostate survived. My friend told me of a woman in Cairo who converted and escaped to Holland before her family caught her.

I wondered, *What would Sheikh Ahmed say if he knew how many doubts I had about Islam? What if I ever left Islam? Would Sheikh Ahmed tell a Muslim to kill me?* These were disturbing thoughts, so I turned the page.

"Mustafa," Sheikh Ahmed said after a few minutes, "you are so serious all the time. What do you do for fun?"

I was glad to turn to lighter conversation. I answered, "I like to play soccer in the evenings, usually with my younger brother. He's one of the fastest runners in our area, so I pass him the ball and he kicks goals."

"I like soccer," said Sheikh Ahmed. "It's a good way to strengthen the body so that you can serve Allah better."

"I also like a game called Siga," I said. "Have you heard of it?"

"I have," he answered, "but I've never played it. It's an old game, is it not?"

"Yes, it goes back to ancient Egypt. Egyptians have passed it down from generation to generation. It has been found carved into the stone roof of a temple that is more than three thousand years old. When I was a kid, I played it at home or on the banks of the Nile River. Would you like to try it?" I asked.

"Why not?" he said. "I don't think people should waste too much time playing board games, but there is nothing else to do on a plane."

Siga is a game you can play almost anywhere with anything. I pulled a piece of paper out of my carry-on bag and drew a grid that was four spaces across and four spaces down, making a total of sixteen spaces. Now all I needed were some playing pieces.

I didn't have any coins with me, but I noticed a lady sitting with her husband across the aisle. She had a large purse, and I was sure that she would have some coins. After a brief conversation, I had five silver coins, five gold coins, and two buttons—everything I needed.

"Siga is a deceptively simple game," I explained to Sheikh Ahmed. "The goal is to capture your opponent's pieces. You do this by sandwiching one of your opponent's pieces between two of yours. Your pieces must be on opposite sides of the piece you are capturing. When you take a turn, you can move one game piece for one space in any direction."

Sheikh Ahmed enjoyed Siga more than I expected. I won the first game easily as he was learning the rules. But by the second game, he was a difficult opponent. On the third game, he nearly beat me.

He said with admiration, "You Egyptians are clever. This game is entertaining, but it also makes you think like a military general. It is an exercise for the brain. I approve."

I thought to myself, *Sheikh Ahmed is a study in contradiction. While he defends suicide bombers and death for apostates, he also plays games and tells jokes.*

A voice from the airplane intercom interrupted us: "Ladies and gentlemen, we are twenty minutes from the Cairo Airport," said the pilot. We both watched out the window as the plane circled once around Cairo, giving us a view of the tightly packed high rises hugging the Nile River. On the west side of the Nile we could see the Great Pyramids of Giza. *This is going to be an interesting week,* I thought.

Chapter 12

The *Amrad* Man

When we got to the baggage claim area, I started looking for my father. I smiled when I saw him, standing there in the midst of a small crowd of relatives and friends. There was my older brother Ibrahim, my younger brother Sayid, my Uncle Hamzi, two friends from primary school, and two friends from Al-Azhar. I didn't really expect my father to come by himself. After all, the return of a *hajji* is a cause for celebration.

My father hugged and kissed me first. "Welcome home, my son. Allah has blessed us by your return." Then he turned to Sheikh Ahmed, "We are honored to have you as our guest."

My younger brother, Sayid, punched me in the shoulder. "It's about time you got back home," he said. "The soccer team needs you back. We've lost two games without you!" After all the introductions and greetings, my older brother announced, "I have good news. I have reservations for all of us to eat at Al-Alphy Restaurant—where they serve Mustafa's favorite food!" Everyone laughed. It was indeed my favorite restaurant in the city. *My family is so good to me*, I thought. *They really want the best for me.*

We all piled into two vans that my father and brother had brought to the airport and honked our way through the congested Cairo traffic until we reached the Al-Azhar campus. The time for the night prayer was only twenty minutes away, so my father announced, "We will pray this time at the mosque of Al-Azhar," and pulled into the parking lot. Sheikh Ahmed was pleased. He said to my father: "Now I see where your son gets his piety. Prayer is better than eating, you could say!"

We hurried through the main gate of the Al-Azhar Mosque, took off our shoes, and entered the huge courtyard. Many people were sitting there, reciting the Quran or just resting on the ground waiting for the fifth time of prayer. We all went to the washing stations and quickly went through the routine. Sheikh Ahmed looked at me with irritation as I did the hair washing by wetting my right hand and wiping it across the front third of my hair. "No, no," he said, "do it this way," as he put water on both of his hands. He then wiped both hands across all of his hair, starting at the front and going all the way to his neck in the back. "That's the way you are supposed to do it," he said firmly. I did as I was told.

When we entered the mosque, we saw a small crowd gathered around an old man sitting in a chair. He was busy teaching them. I didn't think anything of it, and we all started to find our places in the rows for prayer. Then Sheikh Ahmed pulled me aside, "Who is this *amrad* man?" he asked. "How can he be teaching in this place?"

Amrad is an Arabic term for a man who has shaved his beard and moustache. I answered, "This is Sheikh Hakeem, one of the most famous scholars of Islam. He usually sits in the mosque and gives lessons between the fourth and fifth prayers. He is one of several leaders of Al-Azhar who shave their beards. I think they are just more comfortable that way."

"Comfort has nothing to do with the commands of Allah, my son. The commands are to be obeyed. Don't you know that the Prophet said an *amrad* man must never teach or lead prayers? The prayers of an *amrad* man will never go one inch over his head. If this man is leading the prayer, we cannot pray behind him because Allah will not accept our prayers."

Sheikh Ahmed's eyes flashed, and he stood up straight. I thought of my own clean-shaven face and wondered if he knew that I had led prayers many times without a beard. I nervously looked toward the front of the mosque and saw to my relief that a different sheikh was preparing to lead the prayers—a sheikh with a full beard. "Look," I said, "there is someone else who will lead the prayers."

"Allah be praised," said Sheikh Ahmed. "You will need to deal with this other sheikh later."

We slipped into the end of a long row next to my younger brother, and our voices blended with the others in a single, synchronized murmur.

Soon we were back in the vans, joking and talking about how hungry we all were. I noticed some of my friends looking at Sheikh Ahmed's robe and sandals and turban. In Saudi Arabia some Bedouins dressed similar to Sheikh Ahmed, so he didn't stand out too much. Here in Cairo, he looked quite unusual.

After we left Al-Azhar, we drove through Al-Ataba Square to the Imad al-Adin section of Cairo and finally reached the restaurant. The traditional building was a welcome sight to my eyes—painted white with an old-fashioned wooden door and rich curtains in the windows. The waiters greeted us warmly and showed us to the table they had prepared.

My father sat at one end of the table, and he invited Sheikh Ahmed to sit at the other end of the table as our honored guest. We all began looking at the menu, but Sheikh Ahmed didn't pick his up. "I don't read menus," he said. "But I know what I like. Do they serve lamb here?"

"Yes, they do. They make an excellent Egyptian lamb with eggplant. Would you like to try it?"

"Yes," he replied. "I especially like the meat from the shoulder."

"I'm sure the chef will be happy to make that for you," I said. "You know the Prophet liked that meat the best too."

"Of course," he said.

"Should I also order coffee for you?"

"You know how I like it."

We soon had platters full of warm pita bread and bowls of eggplant dip and hummus. The restaurant had some Egyptian music playing in the background, which I had not really noticed until Sheikh Ahmed said, "This is a great song, isn't it?"

I concentrated on the music for a moment and immediately recognized the song by its lyrics: "I love Amr Moussa, and I hate Israel." This lyric repeated twice or three times. Amr Moussa is a household name in the Arab world because he is the secretary general of the Arab World League.

"He's a very popular Egyptian singer," I said. "His name is Shaaban Abdel Rahim. He used to run a dry cleaning shop, and he can't even read or write, but he is famous for this song. I'm glad you like our Egyptian music."

He answered, "I do like it. When I heard it, I felt the deep hatred that Egyptian people have for Israel, and that is a good sign of the influence of Islam over the attitudes of the Egyptian people."

I said, "It's not just in Egypt. Wherever you travel in the Arabic world, you will hear this song at parties, birthday celebrations, or weddings. This song is played all over the Arab countries on national radio and TV stations."

"I know," said Sheikh Ahmed. "But it amazes me that even the countries whose governments have signed peace agreements with Israel allow this song to be played over the national media. What hypocrisy is this?"

"Mustafa, did you hear what happened while you were gone?" asked Sayyid, my younger brother. He didn't wait for me to answer. "You know that little church in the neighborhood next to ours? The policeman assigned to guard the church hit three ladies who were trying to carry bags of sand into the building. They were trying to fix a crack in the floor caused by a water leak somewhere. One of the ladies was Umm William, that Christian lady who is a friend of our mother. Right after it happened, she was so upset that she came straight to our house to tell mother about it."

I was stunned. "Is Umm William hurt?" I asked.

"No," said my brother, "just upset."

My brother had no idea that Umm William was my mother in nursing. All he knew is that she was a friend of my mother.

"I'm so relieved that she wasn't hurt," I said. "Why did the guard do that? Didn't President Mubarek pass a law in 2005 making it legal for churches to repair their buildings?" Mubarek was defying precedent; throughout Islamic history, Christians and Jews living under Muslim governments were routinely barred from maintaining their places of worship.

"Yes," said Sayid, "but this policeman didn't agree with the law."

A new voice joined the conversation. "That's why that policeman has been suspended without pay." It was Sami, one of my friends from primary school who now had a parliament seat in the province where we lived. Sami was somewhat of a renegade among my circle of friends. He started out as a public school teacher, then became a school principal, and finally won a seat in the local parliament in the province where we lived. He was a good leader, but he was a lot more liberal than my family and most of my friends, especially about the role of religion in government.

Sami continued, "The government should not be in the business of harassing its citizens for exercising their rights under the law."

Sheikh Ahmed had been listening closely to the conversation, and now he spoke up. "Who gave the rights to the Christians in the first place? The Prophet never said they had a right to have church buildings that they can use to tempt Muslims to leave the faith."

Sami responded, "I beg your pardon, but these ladies were not trying to make converts. They were only trying to repair an old building. Egyptian law allows them to do that. I believe the Egyptian government needs to protect them even as it protects the Muslim citizens. In fact, you can say I'm crazy, but I think there should be no difference between construction laws for churches and mosques. If Muslims can build new mosques, then I think Christians should be able to build new churches."

Sheikh Ahmed had been listening closely with his lips pressed tightly together. "My son," he said sternly, "what makes you think that the rules of man can override the rules of Allah? The Egyptian government has no right to make a law that is not in harmony with the Quran and the hadith. The Quran says, 'The unbelievers from among the People of the Book and the polytheists are in hellfire and will be there forever. They are the worst of all creation…' (Surah 98:6). Allah does not want these houses of deceit in the land of Islam. You are clearly in error."

Sami looked ready to start a major debate, but when he saw the stress on my face, he decided to let it go. "We must debate this later, when there is more time. For now, let us celebrate Mustafa's return!" None of us brought up the topic at the dinner table again.

As we were eating, Sayid leaned toward me and whispered, "Where did you meet Sheikh Ahmed? He certainly has strong opinions, and he looks like a picture from a history book."

"Actually," I answered, "he found me in a coffee shop. I am fascinated with how well he knows the life of the Prophet, so I invited him to travel with me."

"How long is he going to stay with us?" Sayid asked.

I didn't really know the answer to the question. "Just a few days, I think. He said that he has some friends to meet in Egypt later."

Our food arrived in grand fashion, carried by a small army of waiters. Sheikh Ahmed got his lamb shoulder with eggplant; I had water buffalo kabobs with rice. Other people had chicken kabobs or Egyptian bulti fish from the Nile River cooked with rice and onion. We drank hot tea, coffee, orange juice, apple juice, and mango juice. No one even dreamed about having beer or wine. We enjoyed each other's company, and the hours slipped by. Just before midnight, we left the restaurant, delivering various people to their homes. We finally drove back to my father's house. As we were pulling into the driveway, my father said to me, "Everyone wants you to lead dawn prayer tomorrow at the mosque. Do you think you will be able to do it?"

"I would be glad to," I said.

Inside the house, I showed Sheikh Ahmed to his room, and we all quickly went to bed.

Chapter 13

A Disturbing Dream

Going to bed and sleeping are two different things for me. Even though I was tired, I couldn't sleep. I thought I heard sounds coming from Sheikh Ahmed's room, as if he were talking to someone. I couldn't resist the temptation to put my ear to the wall. He was speaking in a foreign language again, and I was pretty sure that it was Urdu, the major language of Pakistan. Finally, around 1:00 a.m., I fell asleep still hearing the muffled sounds of Sheikh Ahmed's late-night conversations.

In my dreams, I was standing again at Mount Arafat for the *hajj*. I saw Sheikh Ahmed standing at the top of the mountain where Muhammad stood on the day he delivered his final message to the Muslim people. Sheikh Ahmed was shouting loudly, "I am the Prophet; I am not a liar. I am the son of Abdul Mutallib! I am the Prophet; I am not a liar. I am the son of Abdul Mutallib!"

Then Sheikh Ahmed recited from the Quran:

> Ah woe, that Day, to the Rejecters of Truth!
> That will be a Day when they shall not be able to speak.
> Nor will it be open to them to put forth pleas.
> Ah woe, that Day, to the Rejecters of Truth!
> (Surah 77:34–37).

Then he pointed directly at me and said, "Woe to you if you reject the truth. Woe to you."

The sound of knocking at my door woke me up. Sheikh Ahmed was calling loudly, "Prayer is much better than sleep! Prayer is much better than sleep! Prayer is much better than sleep!"

I dragged myself out of bed and went to the bathroom to wash. I started thinking about my dream. *Why would I dream of something like that?* I wondered. *Why would Sheikh Ahmed be standing in the place of the Prophet?* The most troubling thought was, *Why did he accuse me of rejecting the truth? Was my ever-deepening struggle with my faith starting to get the better of me and show?*

I must have been washing slowly because Sayid knocked at the door of the bathroom. "Take your time in there, Mustafa," he said teasingly. "If you are slow enough, I won't have time to do the washing, and then I can pray at home." I knew that he really wanted to pray at home. He wasn't exactly lazy, but he liked to perform his duties the easiest possible way.

"I'm done, I'm done." I answered. "You'll have to pray at the mosque today."

My house was like a nest of bees. Every man and woman was awake, and the men were preparing to go to the mosque for the dawn prayer. As Sheikh Ahmed and I walked down the street to the mosque, I suddenly realized that there was one big problem with my leading the prayer: even though I didn't shave that morning, I still didn't have a full beard. I knew there was only one solution.

"Sheikh Ahmed," I said, "I am supposed to lead the prayers today, but I think everyone would like it if you would be the leader."

"Yes," he said, "I will do it for you. It's a good thing you asked me," he continued, "because if you tried to lead the prayer at the mosque, I would have stopped you. I am sure that you will grow your beard from now on." I felt my face grow red as he said those words. I had been dreading the moment when he finally acknowledged that I was as much an *amrad* man as the clean-shaven sheikh at Al-Azhar.

The mosque was unusually full that morning, and after my older brother gave the second call of prayer, Sheikh Ahmed started to lead. I stood in the first prayer line with my father and two brothers. The prayer leader always recites passages from the Quran, and today Sheikh Ahmed's recitations would be unforgettable.

In the first *raka'ah* Sheikh Ahmed recited *Surah Az-Zalzalah*, "The Earthquake." Sheikh Ahmed spoke in a loud, urgent voice, almost like wailing:

> When the earth is shaken to her (utmost) convulsion,
> And the earth throws up her burdens (from within),
> And man cries (distressed): 'What is the matter with her?'
> On that Day will she declare her tidings:
> For that thy Lord will have given her inspiration.
> On that Day will men proceed in companies sorted out,
> to be shown the deeds that they (had done).
> Then shall anyone who has done an atom's weight of good, see it!
> And anyone who has done an atom's weight of evil, shall see it
> (Surah 99:1–8).

These verses say that on Judgment Day, every good or bad deed a man has done will be placed on the scale, even if it is only the weight of an atom. Then Allah looks at the scale and decides who goes to Paradise and who goes to hell. No one can know for sure what Allah will decide until that day comes. Even the Prophet Muhammad told his people he did not know what would happen to him on Judgment Day. This explains the deep fear of death that Muslims carry because they can never be sure of escaping the hell fire.

Conviction fell on the people. Some had tears coming out of their eyes, and their voices were loud and pleading as they prayed.

For the second *raka'ah* he recited *Surah Al-Qamar*, "The Moon." This was a long chapter, detailing the punishment of those who reject the Quran, from Lot to Noah to the people of Mecca. The combination of these two passages gave a clear message: Serve Allah now, or you will be punished severely on Judgment Day.

He was truly a powerful reciter. After prayer was finished, everyone wanted to greet Sheikh Ahmed before he left the mosque. I kept hearing people talk about the "power of his recitation" and his "passion." They lingered in the mosque, just watching us from a distance.

My father finally asked me, "What are you going to do now?"

I said, "I will take him for a walk along the Nile River to see the morning sun, and then we will go back home to prepare ourselves to go to Al-Azhar University."

My father said, "That's very good. I will go home to help your mother prepare breakfast. We will wait for you to come back, and then we will have breakfast all together."

"Be sure to make coffee," I said. "Sheikh Ahmed loves it."

I was planning to take a leisurely stroll, but in characteristic fashion, Sheikh Ahmed walked briskly, and I nearly had to jog to keep up. We covered the two miles to the river bank quickly. The rising sun turned the waters of the Nile into shimmering, polished gold and made the Great Pyramids of Giza glow like copper. *Nowhere else in the world has a view like this,* I thought with pride.

As he finally slowed down a little bit to enjoy the view, Sheikh Ahmed asked, "What will we do at Al-Azhar today?"

"I am giving my first lecture to my Islamic culture class today," I answered. "I am going to talk about the role of Islamic law in maintaining Islamic culture."

"That is an excellent topic, my son," he said with approval. "I believe Islamic law is the key to restoring the glory of the Muslim world. I have been teaching about Islamic law for years."

"Really?" I said. "Would you like to speak to my class? They can hear me every week, but they rarely hear a teacher from Saudi Arabia."

"As you like," he answered.

As I stared at the water running under the bridge over the Nile, I felt a stab of pain in my stomach from the memory of what I saw under a similar bridge more than twenty years earlier.

Sheikh Ahmed noticed my silence, "What are you thinking about, my son?" he asked.

I wasn't sure how he would respond, but I decided to tell him the story. "When I was ten years old, I often played near a bridge over one of the canals from the Nile. One day I was throwing stones into the water with my brother and some other friends when we saw a black shape in the distance being carried along in the current. 'What's that?' my brother asked me.

"I don't know,' I answered. 'Let's wait and see.'

"As we watched, we could see that the shape was covered in black fabric, and then we saw the pale, bloated legs sticking out from one end of the mass of cloth. It was a young woman's body, floating headless in the waters. My brother screamed. We all started running for our houses, crying for our mothers. Before I could even reach home, I had vomited in the street. I had nightmares for months."

Sheikh Ahmed looked at me seriously. "Why do you think that body ended up in the Nile?" he asked.

"We found out later it was an honor killing. A man accused his wife of having an affair because she went out of the house alone one night without his permission. She said that she had to buy some rice from the grocery store. He was furious with her and insisted that she was lying. In the end, the husband and his brother dragged the wife to the edge of the Nile River and beheaded her, letting her head and body fall in the water."

Now Sheikh Ahmed was stern. "Do you think she committed adultery?"

I answered, "I'm not sure. Maybe she really went to the grocery store. There is no evidence that she had an affair, and it would be hard for her to keep her adultery a secret."

Sheikh Ahmed was not satisfied. "She should not have done

anything to make her husband suspicious," he said harshly.

I answered, "Either way, I think it is sad when a woman is killed this way."

Sheikh Ahmed did not share my remorse. "Mustafa," he said, "you cannot let your feelings get in the way of obeying Islamic law. If she had an affair, then the Prophet said clearly she must be stoned to death. If the Egyptian government does not allow families to enforce Islamic law, then they must take the law into their own hands, as this husband did."

I was shocked by his words. I thought, *If the Prophet were alive today, would he really be this cruel?*

"Sheikh Ahmed," I said, "don't you think the Prophet would feel sad about women dying just because their husbands suspect they had an affair?"

"Yes, he would," he admitted, "but he would still say that obeying the law is more important than feelings."

As the sun inched further up from the horizon, I could already feel the heat of the day building. "I think we had better get back to the house and eat breakfast," I said.

By the time Sheikh Ahmed and I returned to the house, my mother and father had finished preparing the breakfast and called everyone to the table. Most of my family preferred to drink tea with milk, but my mother had prepared a special pot of coffee and placed it at Sheikh Ahmed's place with small pitchers of milk and bee honey. Since we had been awake for several hours, everyone was hungry. We piled our plates with pita and bean dip, scrambled eggs, chunks of feta cheese, and olives. Breakfast with my family was a great way to start any day.

[*Chapter 14*]

The Faithful and the Unfaithful

On the drive from my family's house to Al-Azhar, I had to cross the Bridge of the University over the Nile River. I was just about to drive over the bridge when Sheikh Ahmed said sharply, "Mustafa! What is that at the top of that high rise?" He pointed to a modern glass building on the left-hand side of the road. I didn't need to look up. I knew exactly what he had spotted.

I answered, "It's what you think it is. That is an Israeli flag."

Sheikh Ahmed fumed. "How can the children of monkeys and pigs be permitted to come into Muslim countries and open their embassies and fly their flags in the skies of our cities? Doesn't anybody read the Quran? Doesn't anybody remember how the Jews insulted the Prophet?

> "We have put enmity and hatred among them till the day of resurrection; whenever they kindle a fire for war Allah puts it out, and they strive to make mischief in the land; and Allah does not love the mischief-makers' (Surah 5:64, Shakir)."

I felt a need to defend the Muslims of Egypt. "They do remember the Quran, Sheikh Ahmed, they do," I answered. "The embassy is located at the top of that tall building because of the protests and attacks that the people of Egypt have made against it since it was opened."

Sheikh Ahmed was still indignant. "Then the government of Egypt needs to heed the warning of Allah:

> "O ye who believe! take not the Jews and the Christians for your friends and protectors: They are but friends and protectors to each other. And he amongst you that turns to them (for friendship) is of them. Verily Allah guideth not a people unjust' (Surah 5:51).

"Egypt should not be allied with the children of monkeys and pigs," he finished angrily.

Sheikh Ahmed's attitude was typical of most Muslims who grew up hearing the verses from the Quran that called Jews the children of monkeys and pigs (Surahs 7:166; 5:60; 2:65).

At that moment I was struck with how truly ridiculous it was to say that a group of human beings were the children of monkeys and pigs. How could any sensible person believe this to be true? But millions of Muslims accept this because they believe the Quran is literally true.

As we arrived on campus, Sheikh Ahmed reminded me, "Don't forget about finding that *amrad* professor and telling him that he needs to grow his beard before he teaches or leads prayers anymore. Remember, your duty as a Muslim is to confront any sin that you see. You can't look the other way when you see something done against Islamic law."

I nodded as we walked briskly across campus to my classroom. I was getting used to Sheikh Ahmed being very opinionated. I wondered what he would say to my class.

We quickly reached the building that housed the faculty of Arabic Language and Literature and climbed the stairs to the second floor where I taught in the department of Islamic History and Culture. There were about sixty students already in the room, sitting in the rows of wooden desks. Windows were open to let in fresh air, and I was glad that the heat of the afternoon had not yet set in. All the students were young men in their twenties, and they came from all over the world. Some were wearing African robes, but most were wearing casual Western clothing.

I stood in the front of the room and greeted them, "*Asalaam alaikum* [Peace be upon you]."

The students responded in unison, "*Wa'alaku Asalaam* [Peace also be upon you]."

I gestured toward Sheikh Ahmed. "I am so happy to present you with a special guest speaker today. This is Sheikh Ahmed, who comes to us from Mecca, Saudi Arabia. We met while I was in Mecca for the *hajj*, and he has a deep knowledge of Islam and a passion for our faith. When you see him and hear him speak today, remember that you are hearing and seeing someone very similar to what the Prophet was like in the seventh century."

My students applauded as Sheikh Ahmed came to the podium. He looked at the class with satisfaction.

"I am honored to meet with you—the future scholars and future leaders of the Islamic world," Sheikh Ahmed said. "I see you as better than any son: you are the sons of Islam, and you are the intellectual defenders of our faith. You are chosen ones, honored ones, who do not run from your responsibility before Allah. You refuse to bend to pressure from those who would destroy Islam with their weakness. You would lay down your very lives to defend your faith."

I was surprised at Sheikh Ahmed's words. I didn't expect him to introduce Islamic culture this way. However, I could see that he had captured the students' attention.

He continued, "What is the highest principle of worship in Islam? It is that you do not assign partners to Allah. You do not take the worship that belongs to Allah and give it to any other person or institution. But today—right now—you are surrounded by people who are stealing their worship from Allah and giving it to someone else. Do you know how this is happening?" he asked sternly. My students were perplexed, and I was feeling very nervous.

"I will tell you the answer," he said, "by telling you a story from the life of the Prophet. The Prophet was visited one day by a Christian man named Adi, who was wearing a silver cross. When Adi entered the room, the Prophet was reciting the verse 'They (the People of the Book) have taken their rabbis and priests as lords other than God.'

"Adi tried to correct the Prophet, saying, 'Christians do not worship their priests.'

"The Prophet exposed this lie and explained, 'Whatever their priests and rabbis call permissible, they accept as permissible; whatever they declare as forbidden, they consider as forbidden, and thus they worship their rabbis and their priests.'"

Sheikh Ahmed continued, "The Prophet explained to us clearly that when you obey the laws of a man, you are worshipping that man. Now, let me ask you, O leaders of Islam, whose laws are you following in Egypt? Are these the laws of man or the laws of Allah? If these are the laws of man, and you follow them, then you are worshipping man."

As I expected, they were in shock. They did not expect these strong words. After all, since the early 1960s Al-Azhar was a department of the Egyptian government, and the president appointed the top leaders. If someone at Al-Azhar spoke against the government, he was usually reprimanded by the department leaders. If he continued, he was demoted or fired. That's what happened to Sheikh Omar Abdul Rahman, the blind sheikh who masterminded the 1993 bombing in an underground garage at the World Trade Center. He was a professor at Al-Azhar, but he criticized the government so much that he was fired.

Sheikh Ahmed gazed across the faces in the room. "Maybe you are not sure if Egyptian law and Islamic law are the same. Then let's look at some of these laws and find out.

"What about the law of adultery? Egyptian law says the woman who commits adultery can be imprisoned for up to two years, and the husband can be imprisoned for up to six months. Is this what the Prophet said to do? No! When an adulterer and an adulteress were brought to him, he commanded them both to be stoned to death.

"So," he said sternly, "do you think Islamic law and Egyptian law are the same?"

Most students shook their heads no.

He continued emphatically, "You, O scholars of Al-Azhar, need to expose the difference between the secular law and Islamic law. If your government does not stone the adulterers, then your government is infidel!"

Sheikh Ahmed kept on going, like a crocodile chasing its prey. "The truth is that you cannot compromise the words of the Quran or the example of the Prophet. If you do, then you are idol worshippers, bowing to men who make laws instead of bowing to Allah, the only Law Giver.

"You, O scholars of Al-Azhar, need to tell the Muslim world the truth. They can't keep playing games with Allah and changing Islamic law to suit their desires.

"Let's look at another example—charging interest for loans. The Quran calls this usury and clearly forbids it: 'Allah does not bless usury, and He causes charitable deeds to prosper, and Allah does not love any ungrateful sinner' (Surah 2:276, Shakir).

"So what does Egypt do about charging interest? They set up two systems of banking. The Islamic banks submit to the authority of Allah and refuse to charge interest. But the government banks defiantly charge interest just like any secular bank. This kind of activity denies the authority of Allah and exalts the world financial markets to the status of idols.

"You, O scholars of Al-Azhar, need to tell the Muslim world the truth. If your government is charging interest, then your government is infidel."

Sheikh Ahmed paused, and I turned from him to look out at my students. I saw some of them nodding in agreement or shaking their fists in the air in support. His use of the classical Arabic combined with his message of loyalty to Islam had a powerful effect on their emotions. The only ones who were not caught up in the emotion were the handful of liberal students sitting in the back of the room.

Sheikh Ahmed was just getting warmed up. He spoke with confidence, like someone who was used to telling people what to do.

"There is more. Let's talk about alcohol. Allah knew that the Muslim *ummah* needed to be weaned away from alcohol gradually. So first Allah told Muslims not to pray while drunk (Surah 4:43). Later Allah warned them that alcohol has little to profit them (Surah 2:219). And finally, he made it clear that alcohol is forbidden completely: 'O ye who believe! Intoxicants and gambling...are an abomination, of Satan's handwork: eschew such abomination that ye may prosper' (Surah 5:90).

"Let me ask you this—do you think the Prophet would allow the people of his Muslim community to serve drinks to the non-Muslims who were living among them or visiting? Did he say to the Muslims, 'I know you want to make non-Muslim tourists happy, so go ahead and get alcohol for them'?

"No—that's ridiculous. Allah's Apostle used to strike those who drank wine forty times with shoes or palm branches.

"You, O scholars of Al-Azhar, don't play games with Allah's law. If your government permits alcohol, then your government is infidel.

"And don't forget about robbery. You know what the Quran says: 'As to the thief, male or female, cut off his or her hands: a punishment by way of example, from Allah, for their crime...' There is no excuse for any other form of punishment. The government can't come and say, 'We don't like this. We think it would be better to have jail time.' No! You cannot ignore the words of the Quran. The Prophet said that even if his own daughter were caught stealing, he would cut off her hand.

"You, O scholars of Al-Azhar, need to lead the way. If your government is not cutting off the hand of the robber, then your government is infidel."

I looked at my students' faces after this comment. Most of them were still captivated by Sheikh Ahmed. None of them thought about how horrible it would be to see people's hands cut off in public. None of them considered what it would be like for that person to walk around disfigured and shamed for the rest of his life. I thought to myself, *They don't think; they just listen and repeat what they hear, like parrots.*

Sheikh Ahmed continued, "I have one last point to make, and it is the most important one. There are hypocrite scholars who are trying to cast doubt on parts of Islamic law. They would destroy Islam with their weak interpretations and their crying for tolerance. I'm talking about the judgment upon those who embrace Islam and then turn away from it—the apostates.

"The Prophet himself told you that the blood of a Muslim can only be shed in three cases: as punishment for murder, as punishment for adultery, which we've already discussed, and as punishment for leaving Islam. This law is absolutely necessary to protect the Islamic state."

Sheikh Ahmed pulled a piece of paper out of his brown bag. "Look at this picture," he said. "This is an Afghani man who converted to Christianity."

I stared at the page from the magazine I read on the plane. How did he get that? I never saw him pick it up.

He continued, "The government of Afghanistan was following the laws of Islam and preparing to execute this apostate when the Christians of the world community interfered. Now this man is safe in Italy and can tempt others to leave Islam as well. This is a shame to the Muslim nation.

"You, O scholars of Al-Azhar, must call for the law of apostasy to be put into practice. If your government is not executing the apostates, then your government is infidel."

I felt sick to my stomach. Here I was, questioning whether Islam is the true path to God, and I am hosting a speaker in my classroom who would have me killed if I ever acted on my thoughts. *I am bound to Islam by fear more than faith*, I thought. I wondered about the students in my classroom. Did any of them feel the same way that I did? Even if there were one, it would be suicidal for him to admit it. In the Islamic community, it becomes normal to think one way and speak another.

Sheikh Ahmed finally concluded, "My sons, you are called to worship Allah, not the laws of men. I challenge you to take up the cause of truth and justice. Join the fight to establish Islamic law all over the world, starting with Egypt. Don't let another day go by without confronting the evil in your midst. As the Prophet said, 'If you see something done against Islamic law, you have to change it with your hand. And if you cannot change it with your hand, then change it with your tongue. If you cannot change it with your tongue, then you must change it with your heart. Changing it with your heart is the weakest stage of faith.' Don't be weak. Be strong and bold for your Allah!"

To my relief, Sheikh Ahmed had reached a stopping point. I stood up quickly to make sure he didn't continue to speak. "Sheikh Ahmed," I said, "we cannot thank you enough for speaking to us today. Your powerful lecture will burn in our hearts. It will be a long time before anyone forgets this class."

He replied, "I want you to do more than remember. I want you to take action."

As soon as the lecture was over, the students started talking to each other. I heard them say, "This man is so powerful. He is not like the other professors. He doesn't compromise the faith." Some came to speak with Sheikh Ahmed, asking him when he would visit the class again.

One liberal student asked me quietly, "What is the university going to do when they hear about this?"

I answered, "It will be fine," but I was lying. I knew I would hear from the head of the department about how Sheikh Ahmed complained about the government. I had no idea Sheikh Ahmed was going to speak that way. He seemed to have changed a lot since the time when we were touring Mecca and Medina together.

Sheikh Ahmed thoroughly enjoyed talking with the students. I finally had to announce, "We are out of time. You must let Sheikh Ahmed and me leave now."

Chapter 15

The Woman's Place

I was still in shock from Sheikh Ahmed's strong lecture as we walked to the Al-Azhar outdoor cafeteria for some sandwiches and coffee. As we were looking for a place to sit, I heard a familiar voice calling me, "Dr. Rahal, welcome back. Please come join me." I saw Muhammad Abdu, one of my friends from secondary school, sitting at a table alone. Dr. Abdu was short and stout, and he usually had a smile on his face. He had just become a lecturer in the school of Islamic law, and he was one of the most liberal instructors in his department. He was especially interested in the fair treatment of women. I always enjoyed spending time with him.

"Dr. Abdu," I said. "It's good to see you! We'd be glad to join you."

I introduced him to Sheikh Ahmed as we sat down to eat. "Do you have a class this afternoon?" I asked.

"Yes," he said. "I had a great class planned. I had scheduled Dr. Husain, from the faculty of hadith for a question-and-answer class about Muhammad's perspective on women. Unfortunately, I just saw him, and he said he cannot come because the faculty of hadith is having a big meeting about a new *fatwa* by Dr. Ezzat Atiyah. I was just trying to think of a way to fill his place."

Sheikh Ahmed joined the conversation. "What is a question-

and-answer class?" he asked. "Do the students like it?"

Dr. Abdu looked flattered. "Yes, they do like it," he said. "I have the students write questions in advance, and then I invite an expert on the topic to answer the questions in front of the class. I have excellent attendance on question-and-answer days."

Sheikh Ahmed continued, "I could tell you exactly what the Prophet thought about women. I am very familiar with his life."

Dr. Abdu looked at me questioningly. Sheikh Ahmed was obviously volunteering to speak to his class. I wished that I could warn my friend that Sheikh Ahmed would not give him the answers he wanted, but there was little I could do. I said diplomatically, "Yes, Dr. Abdu, Sheikh Ahmed has a deep knowledge of the Prophet's life. He would do a great job in your class, but I think he is tired since he just finished a lecture to my students. Maybe it would be better some other time."

Sheikh Ahmed spoke up quickly. "I'm not tired. I want to speak to Dr. Abdu's class."

"Then it is decided!" said Dr. Abdu with relief. "Thank you so much, Sheikh Ahmed. My class begins in forty-five minutes," he said as he hurried to finish his sandwich. "I'll meet you there. Dr. Rahal knows where to go."

If only Dr. Abdu knew what he was getting into, I thought.

When we arrived at Dr. Abdu's class, every seat was filled. "I think some of my students brought their friends," said Dr. Abdu.

I thought to myself, *Isn't it interesting that we are about to have a discussion about women, and there is not a single woman in the room.* All of Al-Azhar's female students attended classes at a separate campus where only female students are allowed.

Sheikh Ahmed took a place at a lectern on the left side of the room, and the students gazed with curiosity at his robe and turban. My friend Dr. Abdu went to the lectern on the right side and introduced the class. "Today," he said, "we will celebrate the blessing and liberation that Prophet Muhammad brought to women. In Arabic society before Islam, women suffered discrimination and injustice. Arab culture looked on women as shameful and not good in any way. Some of them even buried their baby daughters in the sand to kill them rather than to raise a girl who might grow up to shame their tribe or community. Muhammad stopped this evil practice and gave the woman her rightful place in Islamic society.

"I want to thank Sheikh Ahmed, from the holy city of Medina, for coming here today. He is a preeminent expert in the life of Muhammad, and we will learn much from him. Sheikh Ahmed, we have already prepared questions to ask you, but first, would you like to greet the class?"

Sheikh Ahmed nodded, "Yes," he said. "Greetings to you—the future scholars and intellectual defenders of our faith. You are chosen ones who will not run from your responsibility before Allah. You refuse to bend to pressure from those who would destroy Islam with their weakness. You would lay down your very lives to defend your faith. I am honored to be with you today."

I saw Dr. Abdu's eyes open wide during Sheikh Ahmed's greeting. It was going to be an interesting class.

"Thank you, Sheikh Ahmed," said Dr. Abdu. "Now I will give you the first question. It is about women in government. Is it acceptable for a woman to hold a high government office, like being a president or a secretary of state?"

Sheikh Ahmed answered with a smile. "Thank you for giving me such an easy question to begin with. The Prophet spoke very specifically about this issue. During the time of the Prophet, the king of Persia died, and the Persian people made his daughter their queen. The Prophet warned, 'Never will succeed such a nation that makes a woman their ruler.' So the answer is very clear: a woman should not take a high government position.

"In addition, a woman should not take a high government position because then she would not fulfill the duties given to her by Allah. The Quran says woman should be at home, guarding her husband's assets. 'Therefore the righteous women are devoutly obedient, and guard in (the husband's) absence what Allah would have them guard' (Surah 4:34)."

Yes, the answer is clear, I thought to myself. *A woman should just stay home.* I thought about my sister, Hoda, who was very intelligent. She excelled in all her academic classes at school, but she never even considered attending college. Instead, my father and mother arranged a good marriage for her, and now she spends her time taking care of her house, cooking her husband's meals, and hoping to get pregnant.

Dr. Abdu looked a little surprised at that answer. I think he hoped Sheikh Ahmed would be more liberal about women's rights. Dr. Abdu flipped through a stack of index cards in his hand. "So you're saying that a woman should not hold a high government office, but what do you say about a woman speaking at a business conference?"

"There weren't many business conferences in the time of the Prophet," Sheikh Ahmed joked. The students laughed. "But I can answer your question because the Quran tells us about the nature of women.

"There is something I need to know," Sheikh Ahmed said to Dr. Abdu.

"Are there men at this business conference?"

"Yes," answered Dr. Abdu. "Men and women."

Sheikh Ahmed spoke confidently. "The answer is that women are not permitted to speak in a meeting where there are men unless there is a great necessity for it."

I looked over at Dr. Abdu. He looked pained. Sheikh Ahmed continued, "There are three reasons: First, a woman should not teach men because men are superior to women in intelligence. Allah explained the intelligence of women when he said, 'The testimony of one man is equal to the testimony of two women' (Surah 2:282).

"Second, the Prophet said if a woman in the mosque wanted to get the leader's attention, she should clap. If the woman must clap and not speak in the mosque, then she should not speak in a conference.

"Third, Allah doesn't allow a woman to raise her voice louder than the voices of men when she worships in the mosque. If the woman must keep her voice lower than the man's in the mosque, then she must keep her voice lower in other public meetings too."

Sheikh Ahmed paused, and Dr. Abdu interjected, "But could you please tell us what should happen if there is a great necessity for a woman to speak?"

"If there is a great necessity for a woman to speak," Sheikh Ahmed answered, "then she must meet three specific conditions.

"First, she must travel with a *dhu-mahram*—a man such as her husband, father, or brother. She cannot travel alone with a man who is not a relative.

"Second, when she speaks at the conference, the men must not be able to see her. There has to be a barrier between her and the people. It can be a curtain or a wall—anything to keep men from seeing her or her face. The Prophet's wives set this example, as it says in *Surah Al-Hazab*: 'And when ye ask (his ladies) for anything ye want, ask them from before a screen: that makes for greater purity for your hearts and for theirs' (Surah 33:33).

"Finally, she is not allowed to soften her voice in a way that would tempt men. Again, the wives of the Prophet are the model as the Quran reveals: 'O wives of the Prophet! you are not like any other of the women; If you will be on your guard, then be not soft in (your) speech, lest he in whose heart is a disease yearn; and speak a good word' (Surah 33:32)."

Dr. Abdu chose the words of his response carefully. "So you say that a woman can speak at a conference as long as she travels with a husband or male relative, stands behind a screen while she is speaking, and does not use a soft voice."

"Yes, that's correct," answered Sheikh Ahmed.

I noticed that almost all the students were responding positively to Sheikh Ahmed, nodding their heads in agreement. Even though Dr. Abdu wanted more freedom for women, most of the students were more conservative.

I knew Dr. Abdu was disappointed with that answer, but he didn't say anything about it. Instead, he approached the topic a new way. "I have another question about what women can do outside of their homes. What would the Prophet say about a group of women going out together for coffee as long as they cover properly and receive permission from their husbands? There would be men in the coffee shop, but the women would not sit with these men."

Sheikh Ahmed responded, "Well, you know there were no coffee shops in the time of the Prophet, but that is a shame because I believe the Prophet would have drunk coffee all the time if he could."

The class laughed at his joke. He was winning them over with his humor.

"But think about the principles the Prophet showed you. Women and men do not kneel side by side in the mosque to pray. Allah showed the Prophet that there must be a screen between the men and the women in the mosque. Allah also told the Prophet to build a special door in the mosque for women only so that women would not be mixed with men as they entered or left the mosque.

"Even when men and women are in public places, they should not mix together. One day the Prophet saw a group of men and women mixed together and walking in the middle of the road. The Prophet said to the women, 'Don't walk next to the men and don't walk in front of the men. Just walk behind them on the edge of the road and they will walk in front of you in the middle.'

"My advice to the Islamic world and the whole world is what Muhammad taught in the seventh century: 'Be careful of the world and of women because the first temptation that the Israelites had was women.' The Jewish people have forgotten this story, and Allah did not tell it to the Prophet in detail. But Allah made it clear that women and men need to stay apart as much as possible."

Dr. Abdu's class about women's rights was slipping away. He didn't even attempt to respond to Sheikh Ahmed's answer. Yet he kept trying to find a way to give women some freedom. He asked Sheikh Ahmed, "We know that the Prophet commanded his wives and the Muslim women of his time to cover their bodies with their veils. Do you think in today's society Allah still wants women to cover the same way?"

Sheikh Ahmed asked the class, "How many of you have been to a wedding party?" Most of them raised their hands.

He continued, "Did you know that the revelation of the veil started with a wedding party and some guests who stayed too long?"

Some students laughed with surprise.

"The Prophet married a new wife and had a wedding party at his house. Even after the Prophet left, the guests were still going in and out of the house. The day after the wedding party, Umar ibn al-Khattib, one of the greatest friends of the Prophet, said, 'Good and bad people were going in and out of your house yesterday. I suggest that you have your wives cover themselves so that they will not be molested.'

"That same day the Prophet received a revelation from the angel Gabriel: 'Tell your wives, daughters, and all the women of the believers to draw their veils over their bodies' (Surah 33:59). So the Quran says quite clearly that 'all the women of the believers' are included. Allah never told women to stop wearing the veil, so it is still a duty today. This is a very easy question."

It's an easy question for men, I thought. *It's a curse for women.* I often felt sorry for women as they walked the streets shrouded in yards of fabric, hardly able to see or breathe. They wear their regular clothing underneath the veil, so they must be desperately hot in the summer. Most women do not realize that their covering started because Muhammad's friend made a comment about men looking at Muhammad's wives during a wedding party.

Dr. Abdu grimly flipped through his stack of index cards looking for new questions. "I have several questions now about marriage," he said. "Here is a question about a Muslim man marrying a Christian or Jewish woman. Is this allowed? If so, can the Christian or Jewish woman continue to practice her faith?"

Sheikh Ahmed replied, "To answer the first part of your question, yes, a Muslim man can marry a Christian or Jewish woman. This happened plenty of times during the life of the Prophet. However, the man always has the leadership of the home, so the children will be raised according to Muslim principles.

"On the other hand, a Muslim woman cannot be married to a Christian or Jewish man because that would make the Christian husband in a position of authority over the Muslim wife.

"Now, for the second part of your question, which was about the wife practicing her faith. The husband should encourage his wife to become a Muslim, but if she refuses, she can keep her own religion. However, the husband should not allow her religion to influence his household. So she can believe in her heart as she will, but her husband may refuse to let her go to the church or synagogue. He should not let her decorate or change the house for non-Muslim holidays."

Sheikh Ahmed paused for effect. "That means no Christmas trees," he said with a smile. The students chuckled.

Sheikh Ahmed concluded, "She can pray at home, but she should pray in a very quiet way so that her voice does not influence anyone in the house."

Dr. Abdu was satisfied with this answer. Not even Dr. Abdu would argue in support of the rights of a Muslim man's Christian wife.

Dr. Abdu turned to the next card. "Here is a question about husbands and their wives having children. What is the correct Islamic opinion regarding birth control?"

Sheikh Ahmed answered, "The concept of birth control has no place in Islamic teaching. The best example is the Prophet and the other messengers of Allah who came before him. The Quran says, 'We did send messengers before thee, and appointed for them wives and children' (Surah 13:38). Because the Prophets had wives and children, the Muslims should also have wives and children. The Quran says, 'These are they whom Allah guided, therefore follow their guidance' (Surah 6:90, Shakir). Allah said, 'Wealth and children are the beauty of this life on earth' (Surah 18:46).

"Having many children is a source of honor for a Muslim family, and it will help Islam by increasing the Muslim population. Look at the Muslims in Europe, how they have large families while the Christians and Jews are having fewer and fewer children. Twenty or thirty years from now, the picture of Europe will be totally different because Europe will be full of Muslims. We will worship our Allah at the Notre Dame Mosque!"

When Sheikh Ahmed said, "Europe will be full of Muslims," many students shook their fists in the air with enthusiasm.

Dr. Abdu checked his watch. "The time has gone by so quickly. This will be our last question." He drew a deep breath before he read from the card in his hand: "What happens if a Muslim woman wants a divorce but her husband doesn't?"

I was impressed that Dr. Abdu had the courage to ask this question. He supported the new Egyptian law that gave women more rights of divorce. However, Al-Azhar had always taught that men had the ultimate decision regarding a divorce except for a few specific conditions. Based on Sheikh Ahmed's attitude in my class, I knew he would put down this question quickly.

Sheikh Ahmed did not hesitate. "I welcome this question. Islamic law says the right of divorce belongs to a man. But he must treat her decently, even in the midst of a divorce because 'men are the protectors and maintainers of women' (Surahs 4:34; 65:1). On the other hand, the woman can only ask for a divorce (*al-khula*) under specific conditions. These are if her husband leaves Islam or he becomes disabled so that he cannot be a husband and father, like being in a coma.

"A wife cannot ask for a divorce just because her husband is taking a second wife, or a third wife or a fourth wife. Allah gave man the right to have up to four wives at the same time, as it says in the Quran: 'Marry (other) women of your choice, two, or three, or four' (Surah 4:3).

"A wife cannot ask for a divorce because her husband disciplines her. The Quran says, 'As to those women on whose part ye fear disloyalty and ill-conduct, admonish them (first), (Next), refuse to share their beds, (And last) beat them (lightly); but if they return to obedience, seek not against them Means (of annoyance)' (Surah 4:34). You can debate about what it means to beat lightly, but the point of the revelation is clear: the husband has the authority to take the necessary steps to make sure his wife does her duties.

"But here is the real issue behind the new divorce laws: Who is worshiping Allah, and who is worshiping human leaders? When you obey a law, you are worshiping the one who made the law. So if you obey the law of Allah, you are worshiping Allah. If you obey the law of a secular government, then you are worshiping man."

A murmur of surprise went through Dr. Abdu's class. Just as he had done in my class, Sheikh Ahmed had directly challenged the Egyptian government for contradicting Islamic law. I could see the students whispering to each other. My friend was taken aback. "Thank you, Sheikh Ahmed," he stammered. "We appreciate your fresh perspective from your point of view."

He's going to hear from the head of his department too, I thought.

Dr. Abdu dismissed the class, and a few students lingered to talk to Sheikh Ahmed, thanking him for coming to the class and asking him to return as soon as possible. Sheikh Ahmed was obviously enjoying himself. Dr. Abdu gave me a look that said, "We need to talk about this later."

Finally, we heard the call for the afternoon prayer, so all of us went to pray in the mosque. When we were finished, Sheikh Ahmed and I walked back to my car. "I'm impressed with the students at Al-Azhar," Sheikh Ahmed said. "They recognize the truth when they hear it."

"No one will ever forget your visit," I agreed. "You captivated the students." To myself I thought, *Sheikh Ahmed is not just a simple tribesman. He can motivate and manipulate people in a very sophisticated way. In my class, he aroused the students' emotions with his powerful command of classical Arabic. It sounded like poetry every time he challenged them by saying, 'You, O scholars of Al-Azhar, don't play games with Allah's law. If your government permits alcohol, then your government is infidel.' But he used a different tactic in Dr. Abdu's class. Though he used classical Arabic for the main part of his lecture, he also used a modern dialect to make frequent jokes. This helped the students to have a favorable impression of him.*

Sheikh Ahmed asked me, "What are the plans for dinner tonight? I would enjoy eating at your house. I love being in the home of a good Muslim family."

Still thinking about his lectures, I answered, "Oh, yes, my mother will be thrilled to have us. There is nothing she likes more than to fill a table with food for a guest. I'll call and let her know we are coming."

Chapter 16

Daring Questions

At dinner that night, we enjoyed light conversation, especially the Egyptian jokes that my younger brother Sayid told. He was the entertainer of the family, and he made a point of listening for new jokes wherever he went. Sheikh Ahmed smiled at times, but he never laughed.

After dinner, my mother and sister turned on the television in the living room. My younger brother was lounging on one of the couches. Sheikh Ahmed and I sat on chairs to the side of the room as he finished drinking another cup of coffee. As my mother flipped through the channels, she stopped at a talk show that we had never seen before called *Daring Questions*. The set looked fresh and modern, and the host was a young, clean-shaven man with a warm smile. He wore a suit jacket and a tie, and he spoke Arabic with a Moroccan accent. He never said that he was a sheikh or an imam, but he said the show would discuss current issues about Islam. He also introduced a guest named Dr. Mark Gabriel as an expert in Islamic history and culture. He was a little older than the host, but also clean shaven and wore a suit and tie. Dr. Gabriel's accent was Egyptian.

"Aren't they handsome," my mother said, nudging my sister.

The host announced, "Tonight we are discussing a new *fatwa* from Al-Azhar University that has shocked the whole world. Here is what happened. A Muslim lady in Egypt wrote a letter to one of the top scholars of hadith at Al-Azhar, Dr. Ezzat Atiyah. She explained that she shared an office with a man at work, and the boss wanted the door to the office closed. Under Islamic law, she is not allowed to be alone in a closed room with a man who is not her husband, her father, or a close relative to whom she could not be married. The professor responded by giving a *fatwa* that stated she could resolve the problem by breastfeeding the man, which, according to Islamic law, turns her into the man's 'mother in nursing.' As his mother in nursing, the woman would be permitted to be in a closed room with the man."

My mother's and sister's eyes opened wide. My younger brother's face got red, and he put his hands over his mouth to cover his laughter. I couldn't believe that I was hearing about a mother in nursing again after talking with Sheikh Ahmed about Muhammad's mother in nursing at the cemetery.

My sister looked at my mother, and my mother looked at me. "My son, is this true, or are these people lying? Did our Prophet really say that?"

Sheikh Ahmed answered her quickly, "Yes, the Prophet said that. I do not understand why anyone would have a hard time with this *fatwa*. The Prophet resolved a problem. This is one of the reasons Allah sent him—to resolve problems people face in their lives."

My mother said to herself softly, "This is something I never imagined."

The program host then aired a clip of a television reporter staring in shock at the newspaper headline about the *fatwa*. This reporter had invited an imam on her television program to give a response. "Does this mean," she pleaded with the imam, "that if I have a driver for my car, I must breastfeed him so that I can ride alone in the car with him? What about the gardener, or the butler? Help me, help me, help me!"

"What is the problem?" the imam said, smiling. "Just do what the Prophet said. The scholar who wrote this *fatwa* didn't establish a new teaching in Islamic law. This man was just a mediator between the Prophet and the Muslim people who are living today. Anyone who objects to this *fatwa* objects to what Allah made lawful."

"Good answer," Sheikh Ahmed said, watching the television intently. I hoped Sheikh Ahmed didn't notice that my mother and sister had covered their faces with their hands in mortification. My brother wasn't laughing any longer.

My mother innocently asked, "Is this the only way the Prophet could solve this problem? There is no other way except this?"

"Let me explain to you the story behind this *fatwa*," said Sheikh Ahmed. "One day a man and his wife came to the Prophet with a problem. Before adoption was abolished, they had adopted a young boy named Salim. Salim had grown up with them as their son. However, after adoption was abolished, he was no longer related to his adopted mother. Therefore Islamic law said he could not be in a room with her alone."

My mother listened to Sheikh Ahmed carefully, but she had a puzzled look on her face. He continued, "This mother came to the Prophet and said, 'Messenger of Allah! We think of Salim as a son and he comes in to see me while I am uncovered. We only have one room, so what can we do about the situation?'

"The Messenger of Allah gave her an answer that solved her problem. He said, 'Give Salim five drinks of your milk and he will be *mahram* by it.' This meant that Salim would become her son in nursing, and then it would be acceptable for him to be with her just as if she were his mother."

The look on my mother's face showed that she was still in shock. Sheikh Ahmed concluded, "My dear sister, many things we do according to our faith, and we do not have the full understanding of it. This is one of those. We accept it because of our faith in Allah and his Prophet."

We turned back to the television program and found the host was giving his concluding statement about the story. "Finally," he said, "I want to talk here a moment about using our intellect when we think about religion. Religion is above the intellect, but it cannot contradict the intellect. This *fatwa* fights against logic. How can one wrong be solved with another wrong? Why would the wrong of a man and woman being in a closed room together be solved by having the woman expose her private parts to the man?"

Sheikh Ahmed frowned. I could see that he was offended, so I asked, "Do you want me to change the channel?"

"No," he said sharply. "I want to see what's going on."

The Apostates

The show host continued, "Our second topic for today is the question, 'Is Muhammad above criticism?' To introduce this question, let's talk about the cartoons that were made and published by the Danish newspaper. You have heard how these cartoons criticized Muhammad. For example, one of them made Muhammad's turban look like an atomic bomb. We disagree with these cartoons because they were not respectful of the Prophet and his teaching."

"That's better," muttered Sheikh Ahmed. "As the Quran says, 'Hatred comes out of their mouths. What they are saying, is just a lie' (Surahs 18:15; 3:118)."

The host continued, "But we are upset by the reaction in the Muslim world that has cost the lives of more than fifty people due to riots. Today we want to talk about whether someone is permitted to draw a picture of Muhammad in a respectful way. First, we want to understand, 'What is an insult to the Prophet?' My guest, Dr. Gabriel, will tell us."

As Dr. Gabriel began to speak, Sheikh Ahmed stared intently at the screen. "The scholars agree," explained Dr. Gabriel, "that every person—Muslim or non-Muslim—who insults the Prophet or takes away from him needs to be killed. This includes saying something against the religion, or Muhammad's lineage, or that Muhammad or the religion is impure. The great scholar Ibn Taymiyyah says that no one should even say the Prophet's clothes are dirty because this is like saying he is impure.

"Furthermore," Dr. Gabriel said, "there is no repentance for insulting the Prophet—neither in this life nor the life to come. This is the harshest punishment in Islam. Even the apostates from Islam have three days to repent and return to Islam and they will be forgiven. Those who commit adultery can find forgiveness by accepting their punishment, even though that means either taking one hundred lashes or being stoned to death. But for insulting the Prophet there is no forgiveness."

The program host interrupted Dr. Gabriel to ask, "What is the justification for this law?"

Dr. Gabriel replied, "In Islamic law, this judgment is called *al-haraba*. The foundation of it comes from the Quran. In *Surah At-Taubah* it says, 'Those who annoy Allah's Messenger will have a painful torment' (Surah 9:61). This verse was talking about people who were mocking Muhammad with words. Also, we have the example of how Muhammad himself dealt with insults and criticism. For example, a Jew named Kaab ibn al-Ashraf was mocking Muhammad with poetry, and Muhammad had his followers assassinate him. So the way Muslims today defend the image of Muhammad is to be expected."

Sheikh Ahmed commented with approval, "Dr. Gabriel has a good understanding, even though he has a Christian name."

"Dr. Gabriel," said the program host, "this is a good time to tell our viewers about a new book that you have written. This book cover is very special because it deals with the issue of what is an insult to Muhammad."

"Yes," said Dr. Gabriel, "I have written a book called *Coffee with the Prophet*. For the cover of this book, I wanted to let people know what the Prophet looked like when he was alive. So I did research about his appearance—his height, his hair, his skin, his clothes, his jewelry, and even his shoes. I took all this information to a professional artist, and I would like to show you the picture that he produced."

At that moment, the picture of a book cover appeared on the TV screen. It showed a man with a brown robe, a turban, and sandals sitting in a modern coffee shop and talking with Dr. Gabriel.

"O Allah," my mother exclaimed. "Is this the Prophet?"

My sister gasped, "I never dreamed of what the Prophet would look like!"

We all turned to look at Sheikh Ahmed. It was impossible not to see the resemblance.

"Sheikh Ahmed," my mother exclaimed, "you look just like the picture!"

Sheikh Ahmed smiled. "I respect this drawing," he said. "The one who did it was not trying to mock the Prophet. He just wanted to show a good image of what the Prophet looked like."

I was surprised at his tolerant attitude. "Sheikh Ahmed," I said, "many scholars say that the Prophet prohibited all images of living things, such as people and animals. There is a hadith that says, 'Verily the most grievously tormented people amongst the inhabitants of Hell on the Day of Resurrection would be the painters of pictures.' Scholars say that if Allah prohibited pictures of people, then he prohibited pictures of Muhammad as well."

Sheikh Ahmed answered, "Yes, my son, the Prophet said that. But do you know the story of when the Prophet conquered Mecca and cleaned the idols out of al-Ka'aba? He spared a statue of the Virgin Mary with Jesus and a painting of the prophet Ibrahim. So Muhammad did not mean that all images are prohibited."

He continued, "But what I want to know is how a Christian man learned such detailed information about Islam and the appearance of the Prophet."

At that moment, the program host answered Sheikh Ahmed's question. The host turned to Dr. Gabriel and said, "You were a lecturer at Al-Azhar, and the story of your conversion to Christianity has been reported around the world. How do you think Al-Azhar will react to this book? What will your family and friends say when they see this program?"

"This man is an apostate!" exclaimed Sheikh Ahmed in disgust.

Dr. Gabriel explained, "My family is going to have a hard time with this, of course. But I want to tell them that I love them and that I have peace in my soul. As far as Al-Azhar, they have already denied my existence, so I think they will continue to do more of the same."

My mother gasped, talking to Dr. Gabriel through the TV screen. "How could you do that? Where are you now? My heart goes out to your poor mother."

My brother asked me, "He's supposed to be from Al-Azhar. Have you ever heard of him?"

"No," I said, "but he talks like someone from Al-Azhar."

We turned our attention to the TV again. Dr. Gabriel said, "The hardest thing in my life has been to leave my family and my country behind. I cry for them every day. But right now there are 15 million men and women who have left Islam, especially after the radical attacks against the United States on 9/11. We former Muslims need to support each other, so I've started a group called the Union of Former Muslims to defend our rights as human beings to choose our religion."

Sheikh Ahmed didn't like hearing about this group at all. "Do you know why a group like this can exist today?" he exclaimed. "It's because of the disastrous day when the caliphate was destroyed in 1924. When Muslims have their own caliphate, then the caliphate will take care of a conversion movement like this. Look at Abu Bakr, who became caliph after Muhammad's death. Immediately a group of new Muslim converts refused to pay the charity tax, which meant that they were apostate because they had denied a pillar of Islam. Abu Bakr sent his best general to fight them, and he killed eighty thousand of these apostates in three months [the Ridda Wars]."

I wondered, *Why does this union bother Sheikh Ahmed so much? They are only a handful of people compared to 1.3 billion Muslims in the world today. Would an Islamic state really need to seek them out and kill them the way Abu Bakr killed the ones who left Islam in the seventh century?*

It was definitely time to change the channel. "Sayid," I said loudly, "isn't there a soccer game that you want to watch?"

He caught the hint. "Oh, yes, Mustafa, I almost forgot," and he changed the channel.

Sheikh Ahmed looked at me sternly. "Mustafa, you need to find out what is going on with that program. It is very dangerous. Weak Muslims could be lead astray by their questions and answers. Are you sure you've never seen it before?"

"No," I assured him. "I've definitely never seen it before."

Trapped

After the tension of seeing the talk show on the television, I thought it would be good to get outside. Sheikh Ahmed's demands were beginning to make me feel uncomfortable and guilty, and I just wanted to avoid controversial issues. "Would you like to come up to the roof with me and play some Siga?" I asked Sheikh Ahmed. "I'd like to relax in the fresh air."

The roof was my favorite part of the house. Like many of the roofs in Egypt, it was flat and had a concrete floor and a wall along the edge. On our roof we had two wicker tables with glass tops surrounded by chairs as well as some couches with cushions. The floor was softened with some area rugs, which were faded from the sun but still in good condition since it rains only once or twice a year in Egypt.

I picked up a nice Siga game set from my room, and then Sheikh Ahmed and I walked up the stairs to get to the roof door on the fourth floor. Sheikh Ahmed relaxed a little and joked, "I'm going to beat you this time."

As we put our game pieces on the board, I looked at Sheikh Ahmed, wearing the same robe and turban he wore the day I met him. He was fully committed to Islam without any hint of doubt. He knew more about the life of the Prophet than anyone I'd ever met. But the more I learned about the Prophet, the more doubts I had. Being with him added to my knowledge, but it was ultimately tearing away at my faith. Maybe I just wasn't trying hard enough to please Allah.

I definitely wasn't trying hard enough to beat Sheikh Ahmed at Siga. "I've captured another one of your men," Sheikh Ahmed announced.

"I'm just daydreaming, I guess," I explained. "Can I ask you a question?"

"Of course, my son. I am eager to hear all your questions."

"What pleases Allah the most?"

"That's a good question," he replied. "Allah is pleased with all five pillars of worship—confessing the faith, praying five times a day, fasting during Ramadan, giving to the poor, and doing the *hajj*. But what pleases Allah the most goes beyond that. It is when a Muslim gives everything to fight in the cause of Islam."

I tried to concentrate on the Siga game so that I wouldn't have to look at Sheikh Ahmed directly. I was afraid of the direction this conversation was headed. "Are you talking about jihad?" I asked.

Sheikh Ahmed answered, "Yes. As the Prophet said, 'Jihad is the head of Islam.' If you try to take away jihad, you cut off the head of Islam. Without jihad, Islam would never have been established and never survived. The Prophet could have spent his whole life in Mecca, being quiet and tolerant, but he would never have established the authority of Allah the way he did with his military in Medina. Jihad is far more important than all the five pillars put together."

"Are you saying that to please Allah I must join a jihad group?" I asked.

"Yes," he said. "You need to support those who are most committed to Allah and his Prophet. I am in touch with leaders of these groups all over the world, and I will connect you with the right people." I took a deep breath. For the first time, I felt afraid of Sheikh Ahmed.

"Do I need to die as a martyr in jihad to please Allah?" I asked hesitantly.

Sheikh Ahmed responded firmly, "No. You are not called to be a martyr. That would be a waste of your position and your education. Your life is more valuable than your death." I couldn't believe how calmly Sheikh Ahmed was speaking about the value of my life. *What if I were a normal Muslim, like my brother Sayid? Would that make me disposable?*

He continued, "Mustafa, even your name means 'chosen one.' Allah chose you to study Islam deeply from a young age so that you could serve him with words. He has called you to fight in the classrooms of Al-Azhar. This is your duty, Mustafa. You must fulfill it."

I knew I had to say something at this moment or Sheikh Ahmed would know that my faith was wavering. I said emphatically, "Nothing is more important to me than serving Allah," and this was the truth. I wanted to lay down my life for the true Allah of heaven. I just wasn't sure the true God of heaven was the same as Muhammad's God or the God of the jihad groups.

Sheikh Ahmed looked at me suspiciously but answered, "You have spoken well. Now you need to act on what you say."

I thought, *This is a dangerous game that I am playing. I feel as trapped as one of these Siga pieces.*

I looked down at the Siga game board. Sheikh Ahmed had captured all but three of my pieces. It was only a matter of time before I lost—unless I stopped playing the game. The crackling sound of the neighborhood loudspeakers interrupted my thoughts. The call to sunset prayer rang out through the streets. "We'll have to finish this game tomorrow night," said Sheikh Ahmed as we went downstairs to wash before going to the mosque.

My brother Sayid was still on the couch as we started out the front door. "Sayid," Sheikh Ahmed asked him, "why aren't you coming to prayer?"

"I'm not feeling well," said Sayid. "I think I'm getting a cold. I'm going to pray at home tonight."

"Don't you know what the Prophet said about those who neglected the prayer?" Sheikh Ahmed said with irritation. "He said, 'The heaviest prayer on the Muslim hypocrites is the night prayer and the dawn prayer, and if they knew what was in these two prayers, they would even crawl to them.'"

If I were Sayid, I would have been insulted, but he just shrugged it off with a smile. "Sheikh Ahmed, I'm surprised at you," he said. "Do you want me to spread my germs to the whole neighborhood?"

Sheikh Ahmed and I stayed at the mosque between sunset and night prayers, talking to my father and older brother as well as our neighbors. As we all walked home, I started thinking about what I would do with Sheikh Ahmed the next day. I didn't have any classes to teach, and I really didn't want him speaking to any students at Al-Azhar anyway. I was already going to get in enough trouble. Then I thought of the library.

"Sheikh Ahmed," I said as we were preparing to go to our rooms, "I'd like to take you to the Al-Azhar library tomorrow. It has one of the finest collections of Islamic literature in the world."

He looked at me with an amused expression on his face. "My son," he said, "do you realize that I cannot read or write?"

I was embarrassed that I hadn't figured that out. No wonder he never looked at menus and didn't want to read a magazine on the airplane. I stammered, "No, I didn't see that. You know the Quran and the life of the Prophet so well, I just assumed..."

"It's no problem," he said. "I am not offended. I would like to see this library and find out what resources the great scholars of Al-Azhar have. If I see something of interest, you can read it to me."

"I would be glad to," I replied, feeling relieved that my library plan would still work.

Chapter 19

Family Crisis

When Sheikh Ahmed saw me in the morning, the first thing he said was, "I see you are growing your beard."

I had two days' worth of stubble, but he was pleased.

"Good for you, my son. You are putting action to your words. You need to do that in other areas too."

Sayid never came out of his room for the call to prayer. I hoped that Sheikh Ahmed didn't notice.

After the dawn prayer, we walked back to the house with my father, who said, "Mustafa, I'd like to show Sheikh Ahmed our furniture factory today."

"That is an excellent idea," I said, realizing that it would be a good way to pass the time. "We could go there this morning on our way to the university."

"That would be fine," he agreed.

When we arrived back at the house, Sayid was just coming out of his room. He looked at Sheikh Ahmed and quickly explained, "I prayed in my room."

Sheikh Ahmed frowned. "Sayid, you are not sick enough to stay home from prayer. Do you know what the Prophet said to Muslims who skipped prayer? He said, 'I should have gone to your houses and burned them down with you inside.'"

I couldn't believe how harsh Sheikh Ahmed was with Sayid. "I'm sure Sayid will go to the mosque for the next prayer," I said, and then turned to Sayid and asked, "Are you feeling any better?"

"Yes," he said. "I took some medicine for the cold."

I felt a sudden strong urge to spend the day with my brother. We hadn't spent much time together since I got back from the *hajj*. "Would you like to go to the library with Sheikh Ahmed and me?" I asked.

"You know I'm not a bookworm like you, Mustafa. But I think I would like the library more than working at the furniture store, so I'll go with you."

My father left for the factory early, and Sheikh Ahmed, Sayid, and I were soon on our way to meet him there. I felt my father's pride as we drove up to the well-kept cement building with the words *Al-Rahal Fine Furniture* written in Arabic on the sign above the door.

He came outside to escort us into the building. "Here is the place where the carpenters do the first cuts on the mahogany," he said loudly over the sound of table saws. "And here is where the best woodcarvers in Egypt carve out the wood." Two craftsmen were hard at work with chisels and sandpaper, making the intricate carvings of flowers and scrollwork that my father's furniture was known for. Another part of the factory was reserved for wood staining and finishing. Finally, the pieces were assembled and the upholstery was tacked on.

My father was known for the quality of his work, and the best homes and businesses in Cairo were furnished with his products. My older brother helped him with the daily tasks of running the company. My younger brother did various odd jobs.

"Sayid," my father said when we had finished touring the building, "a large order came on the fax machine overnight. It has to be delivered today, and one of my delivery men is sick, so I need you to work on deliveries today."

Sayid answered, "Actually, I was going to visit the library with Mustafa today. Do you really need me?"

My father answered, "I'm sorry. I really do."

I told my brother, "It's OK. Work here today, and I'll see you tonight at dinner. We can go somewhere together tomorrow." None of us had any idea what a disaster this simple decision would cause.

On the way to the Al-Azhar campus, I drove past the Israeli Embassy again, and Sheikh Ahmed cursed it vigorously. When we arrived on campus, I first took Sheikh Ahmed to see the beautiful room in the Al-Azhar Mosque where the library used to be kept. The old library was famous for the beautiful crimson, purple, and green designs painted on the domed ceiling. Then we took the five-minute walk to the current library location. Even though it was not even nine o'clock in the morning, the temperature in the sun felt like almost 100 degrees Fahrenheit (38 degrees Celsius), and the paved sidewalk shimmered with the heat. *It's a tough day to deliver furniture,* I thought.

The Al-Azhar Library is a place where scholars from around the world come to study a huge collection of books about the life of Muhammad, Islamic law, Islamic history, and Islamic literature. It is particularly famous for its collection of ancient scrolls from the earliest days of Islam. Before the days of the computer, the university had photographed the scrolls and placed the images on microfilm.

"Sheikh Ahmed," I said, "would you like me to show you how you can look at some of the oldest Islamic documents in the world on microfilm?"

He looked puzzled, but he replied, "As you wish."

I found the microfilm that contained the letters Muhammad sent to the first governor of Egypt and the king of Persia (now Iran), calling for them to convert to Islam. When I had the image in focus, I told him to look into the viewfinder.

"O Allah!" he exclaimed. "How did you get this? I can see the seal of the Prophet himself at the bottom of the letters. He used his silver ring to put this seal on all the important letters that he sent out. And the caliphs after him, until Uthman, used the ring to seal their letters too."

Sheikh Ahmed could hardly contain his excitement. "Which letters are these?"

"These are the letters Muhammad sent to Egypt and Persia," I answered.

"Allah be praised!" Sheikh Ahmed exclaimed enthusiastically. "Show me more documents like this!"

I showed him a copy of the two agreements between Muhammad and the Quraysh tribe of Mecca (known as the First al-Aqaba and the Second al-Aqaba.) After some searching, I also found a microfilm with a few pages from the Uthman Quran, the authorized collection of the Quran approved by the Uthman, the third caliph. After he established the authorized version of the Quran, Uthman gathered all other versions and destroyed them.

I spent hours showing Sheikh Ahmed the ancient manuscripts until it was time for the noon prayer. After prayer, we went to a little restaurant on Al-Azhar Street where we could get the one of the university's most popular lunches—a plate of rice and macaroni seasoned with onion, tomato, hot pepper, and chickpeas. It's the original "fast food" of the area. You just pay, the worker spoons the food onto a plate, and you grab it and go.

After lunch and noon prayer, I gave Sheikh Ahmed a tour of the hadith section of the library. He admired the long rows of shelves filled with heavy books with deeply embossed covers. At his request, I pulled out some volumes randomly and read to him. He smiled when I mentioned different people by name.

Compared to the lectures the day before, this was a very peaceful day. *He is quite a pleasant person as long as you don't disagree with him,* I thought.

We did the afternoon prayer at Al-Azhar Mosque, and we might have done the sunset prayer there too, but both of us wanted to get back to the house in time to eat the dinner my mother was preparing.

We arrived back at my house right before dinnertime. My mother and sister were in the kitchen, and I could smell the results of their day of cooking.

I went into the kitchen and gave my mother a kiss. "You spoil us with your cooking," I said.

"Yes," said Sheikh Ahmed, "thanks to you I think the belt of my robe is getting shorter!" Even though he was very harsh about some people, Sheikh Ahmed was always nice to my mother.

She smiled and said, "Your father and brothers should be here soon, and then we'll eat." But when they arrived five minutes later, we knew something was wrong. My father and older brother held Sayid's arms as they led him into the house. His face was red, and he was gasping for air.

"Sayid, what is wrong?" my mother cried out, rushing over to him.

"It's OK," he said. "It's OK. I'm just really thirsty."

My older brother whispered, "He was like this when he came back from delivering furniture."

Sayid sat down in a chair at the dinner table. My mother quickly brought him a tall glass of water. With his hand trembling, he drank it all. Then he asked for some juice. My mother practically ran back to the kitchen and returned with a glass full of juice.

"There. I'm fine, Mom. I just need to lie down," he reassured her.

I stood beside him. "Let me help you to your room," I said. When I touched his arm, his skin was burning hot and dry. My father and I held him up between us and led him to his room. My mother and sister were right behind us. "Sayid, my son," my mother moaned. "O Allah, help us."

A few minutes later, Sayid yelled from his room, "I need a bucket!"

The hours dragged by as my brother grew worse. He drank water and juice, but he would vomit it back up. He was disoriented, too. "Mustafa, where are you?" he called out. "I'm ready to go to the library."

By 10:00 p.m. the wail of the ambulance siren was outside our door. As the paramedics carried Sayid out of the house on a stretcher, I walked next to him, holding his hand. "You'll be OK," I said, trying to sound confident. Sayid's eyes were glassy, and he didn't answer.

My mother and father got in the front of the ambulance with the driver. As the paramedics slid Sayid into the back of the ambulance, I recited the Quran's verse of healing to him: "If Allah touch thee with affliction, none can remove it but He; if He touch thee with happiness, He hath power over all things" (Surah 6:19). I started to climb in the back of the ambulance with Sayid when a paramedic stopped me gently. "I'm sorry," he said, "we can only let your father and mother go to the hospital."

Sheikh Ahmed stood with me in front of the house as the ambulance sped away. "We cannot question Allah's will," he murmured. I felt tears coming to my eyes as I tried to stop my mind from racing ahead to what might happen. I felt utterly helpless—and afraid. Sheikh Ahmed looked restless, as if he needed to go somewhere or do something.

"Sheikh Ahmed," I said, "I'm going to sit on the roof for a while because I know I won't be able to sleep. You are welcome to rest in your room or do whatever you would like to do."

"Mustafa," he said. "I will join you in a few minutes. I want to talk with you."

"Thank you," I replied. "I need someone to be with me tonight."

Explanations

Even on the rooftop, the heat from the day still hung over the city and no breeze stirred the air. I thought about Sayid in the hospital. I knew he probably had sunstroke; he had all the symptoms. Tonight could decide whether he would live or die. As I waited for Sheikh Ahmed, I knelt on one of the rugs on the cement floor and started to plead with Allah for my brother. "O Allah, have mercy," I begged. "This cannot be Sayid's destiny." Tears slid down my cheeks.

Finally I heard Sheikh Ahmed's voice. "Mustafa," he said. "I am here."

I looked up at him. "I am sorry about Sayid," he said. "His condition is most unfortunate."

"Thank you," I said, looking up at him awkwardly as I knelt on the floor.

Sheikh Ahmed gestured toward some chairs. "Can you get up and sit with me for a few minutes? I need to tell you something."

I got up off my knees and sat in the chair as he sat across from me. "What is it?" I asked.

"I've been called away to meet with someone else in Egypt," he said matter-of-factly.

"What?" I said. "Meet with someone else? I don't understand."

"I've already stayed longer than I normally do."

I was really confused. "I don't know what you mean. But you can't go now. We need you to help us pray for Sayid to recover."

"Mustafa," he said, looking at me. He seemed sympathetic but impatient. "Do you remember the story of the Prophet's son Ibrahim? When the boy was two years old, he became deathly ill. The Prophet held him in his arms, begging Allah to touch him and heal him, but Ibrahim died. If I could cause Allah to heal Sayid, I would do it. But Allah has not given me the authority to do that—not with Ibraham and not with Sayid. I am but a slave of Allah, just like you."

"Before I go," Sheikh Ahmed continued, "I need to tell you something about me, but if you tell anyone, Allah will end your life instantly. Do you swear in the name of Allah that you will not repeat what I am about to tell you?"

"I swear in the name of Allah," I answered, feeling completely bewildered. *Why was he saying something like this when my heart was breaking for my brother Sayid?*

Sheikh Ahmed continued: "Do you remember the drawing of Muhammad on the television program? Do you remember how much it looked like me?"

"Yes," I nodded.

Then he looked at me directly in the eyes and said, "I am the one I look like. I am the Prophet."

He paused to see my reaction. All I could do was stare at him. I felt as if something had exploded in my brain. I never imagined this. I stammered, "How can this be? How can I know that you are really the Prophet? I don't understand."

Sheikh Ahmed explained calmly, "Allah has given a powerful

protection over my image. As I said fourteen hundred years ago, 'When anyone sees my image, it is as if he had actually seen me.' Allah will not allow Satan or any demon to masquerade in my image. This is a great blessing from Allah to Muslims because when a Muslim sees my image, he can be sure that he is seeing me."

He paused to let me process what he was saying. Then he added, "Mustafa, this is the truth: I look like the Prophet because I am the Prophet.

"Look," he said, holding up his hand. "Here is the silver ring that I made for myself fourteen hundred years ago." He slid the thick ring off his finger. "See the inscription?" He handed the ring to me. There were three lines of Arabic words deeply etched into the outside of the ring:

> Muhammad,
> the Apostle
> of Allah.

"I used this ring to seal the letters that I sent to the kings and leaders in Arabia, telling them to submit to Islam," Sheikh Ahmed explained.

I was stunned, but I automatically began thinking about my studies of Islamic history. I had learned about the ring, but I also remembered something else. "Sheikh Ahmed," I challenged him timidly, "wasn't this ring lost?"

"Mustafa," he said, "your mind is always sharp. Yes, my companion Uthman, who was the third caliph after my death, had the ring. He was sitting on the edge of a well playing with it when it fell into the water. They searched for three days and drained the well, but they could not find the ring. Do you know why they couldn't find the ring?"

I could not answer.

"They couldn't find the ring because Allah returned it to me," he said. "Allah brought it to me in my grave and told me, 'This ring was yours when you walked the earth. I give it to you now, and with it you may walk the earth again to serve me as I command.'

"Allah gave me two missions. First, I am sent to those Muslims whose faith is wavering. Second, I support those Muslims who are most committed to Islam and willing to give their lives for their faith."

"You mean the jihad groups?" I asked.

"Yes," he answered. "All those groups who have fought for Allah in the past fourteen hundred years."

"What do you do with these groups?" I asked, my curiosity overcoming my disbelief.

"I give them ideas. I give them inspiration. I am in contact with leaders all over the world. Do you remember when you heard me talking at night in different languages? I was talking to some of those leaders. You asked me how I learned those different languages, but I didn't give you the complete answer at the time. In the seventh century, Allah gave me the ability to recite the Quran in seven different dialects so I could preach Islam to the people. Since then, Allah has allowed me to speak in any language that I need in order to communicate with the believers."

My mind was spinning. "If you are the Prophet, why would you come to me?"

"Mustafa," he said, "you don't have to pretend any longer with me. Allah knows your faith is wavering. He sent me to bring you back to the straight path. He has heard the prayers and cries of your mother and father and uncle since you were a little boy, begging Allah to protect you so that you would not stray away from the truth."

I tried to protest, "I'm not pretending. I am willing to give my life for Allah. I have fulfilled every duty as faithfully as any human being could."

He interrupted me. "Mustafa," he said, "I know about the

Christian lady who nursed you as a baby."

I felt my heart beat faster as he said these words. I stared at the ground as he continued, "Her name was Umm William, and she is a friend of your mother to this day. Your parents let her nurse you because you wouldn't nurse from any other woman."

My heart felt as if it were trembling in my chest. *How could he know that? What was he going to do to me?*

"Don't be afraid of me," he said. "I am not here to judge you. Allah will do that. I am here as a warner. You are at a crossroads. You must decide what path you will take. Allah has chosen you and prepared you to fight for him as a scholar at Al-Azhar. If you reject that duty, then you know the consequences."

I knew exactly what he meant by consequences. He made it perfectly clear in his lecture to my class about apostasy.

"Mustafa," he said, "we are about to go separate ways, but I need to give you something." He reached into the rough brown sack that he always carried with him and felt around inside it for a few moments, as if he were trying to find something in particular. He finally found what he was looking for. "Put out your hand," he commanded. My hand trembled as I held it in front of me. He reached toward me and placed a smooth silver object in my palm. It was a cell phone.

I stared at it in astonishment.

He explained, "This phone is the only way you will ever be able to contact me again. It will only work for one phone call, and you can use it day or night. If I do not answer, leave a message, and I will call you back. We will be able to talk for twenty minutes before the connection is cut off. The phone will not work again after that."

I gripped the phone in both hands. "Do you talk to a lot of people with cell phones?" I asked. "I heard you almost every night."

"Yes," he said. "Allah embraces any new technology that will help the cause of Islam."

I desperately wanted to know more about this phone I gripped in my hands. "Do you have a lot of cell phones in your bag?" I asked. "Are they all the same?"

"No," he said, "I give different phones to different people. Some of them are so I can communicate with the great leaders around the world who are fighting the jihad to restore the caliphate. Others are for ones like you. You do not need to know any more than that."

"I don't know what to do," I said, feeling panicky. "When do you want me to call you? Do you want me to tell you what happens with Sayid?"

"Whatever you like," he answered. "Allah will not allow us to meet face-to-face again, but he does give you one phone call."

Sheikh Ahmed stood up briskly, placing the strap of his brown bag over his shoulder. I stood with him.

"Are you leaving now?" I asked in shock.

"Yes," he said. "Allah does not permit me to stay any longer."

"But, what about Sayid…" I pleaded.

He said firmly, "My deepest desire is for your brother to recover and live to serve Allah."

"Can't you do anything for him?" I said, trembling.

"I can't," he said flatly. "You know that I am only a slave of Allah, just like you. And now Allah has told me to go. All I can say is to seek refuge in the words of Allah. Remember the Verse of the Chair (*Ayat al-Kursi*); it is the most powerful. But more important, think about yourself and your duty."

He immediately turned away from me and strode across the rooftop to the stairway. He never looked back, and I watched the door swing shut behind him. I was alone.

I looked at the silver cell phone in my hand. The stars, and the chairs, and the roof started spinning, and a wave of heat engulfed my body. As I stuffed the cell phone in my pocket, I heard a buzzing sound in my ears, the sky went black, and I fainted.

Chapter 21

A Dark Mosque

When I woke up, I was lying face down on the floor. My left knee was scraped and I could feel a lump on my forehead, but I didn't care about that. My brain was so full of questions that I felt as if it would explode. *Was Sheikh Ahmed really the Prophet? How is it even possible? Or was he lying? Was he just a crazy old man with delusions of grandeur?*

If he were the Prophet, how could he leave us while Sayid might be dying? Why didn't he help us pray?

Either way, I thought, *I've got to think about my brother now. What if Sayid died?* He was a good person—fun-loving and kind. But he wasn't perfect. He missed prayer times. He didn't always give money for the poor. He never had a chance to do the pilgrimage. Would his grave be a little Paradise or a place of torture? None of us knew.

Muhammad only told us that two angels were assigned to each person. One angel would write down all the person's good deeds, and the other would record all the bad deeds (Surah 50:17). The angels would report to Allah on Judgment Day, and then Allah would decide whether to send the person to Paradise or to hell.

I sat for a few minutes, rubbing the lump on my forehead and feeling overwhelmed. Then I knew what I had to do. I limped down the stairs as quickly as I could, grabbed my keys out of my room, and went out onto the street. The neighborhood was quiet, deserted, and inky black. I noticed that the streetlights were not working as I half-walked, half-ran toward the neighborhood mosque where my family and I prayed five times a day. I arrived at the mosque shortly after midnight, pulled my keys out of my pocket, and unlocked the door. I flipped the light switch on and nothing happened. I realized that the electricity in the mosque wasn't working.

The darkness inside the building was relentless. Whether my eyes were opened or closed, I could not see anything. But I knew the building as if it were my own room at home. So I put my left shoulder against the wall and my left hand on the wall in front of me and felt my way to the platform where the imam stood to lead prayers. I found my way to the little closet under the platform and opened it. Groping with my hand, I located a candle and a book of matches inside. I lit one candle, found a stand for it, walked to the center of the mosque, and sat down on the ground, placing the candle next to me.

In a loud voice, I spoke one of Muhammad's most famous prayers: "I seek refuge in the perfect words of Allah from the evil of what he has created." My voice echoed off the walls. I shouted it again: "I seek refuge in the perfect words of Allah from the evil of what he has created." My voice was the only life in the room.

All the Muslim scholars say that to "seek refuge in the perfect words of Allah" means to recite the Quran. *I will recite for Sayid,* I said to myself. *I will recite with every bit of strength that I have.* First, I recited the Verse of the Chair (*Ayat al-Kursi*):

> There is no god but He,
> The Living, the Everlasting,
> Slumber seizes Him not, neither sleep,
> To Him belongs all that is in the heavens and the earth.
> Who is there that can intercede with Him, except by His
>   leave?
> He knows what lies before them and what is after them,
> And they comprehend not anything of His Knowledge

> save as He wills.
> His throne comprises the heavens and the earth,
> The preserving of them fatigues Him not,
> And He is the All-High, All-Glorious
> (Surah 2:255).

Then I recited more passages and chapters from all over the Quran, but after I finished each part, I would repeat *Ayat al-Kursi* and Muhammad's prayer. I clung to the possibility that my words would please Allah and move him to answer my prayers and the prayers of my family.

I tried not to think about Sheikh Ahmed. I didn't have the emotional strength to do it. In fear and desperation for the life of my brother, I focused on my reciting.

After three hours, I picked up the candle and went back to the wall of the mosque. When I had touched the wall with my hand and knew where I was, I blew out the candle and put the stand on the ground. In the dark, using my hand to guide me along the wall, I walked from corner to corner of the mosque, crying and praying and pleading with Allah. "O Allah, O Allah! Hear me tonight. For the sake of your messenger, Muhammad, hear my prayer. I have poured out my life like water seeking after you, O Allah. Hear my prayer tonight. Touch Sayid; heal Sayid; heal my brother."

The tears ran down my face, but I felt nothing. I saw nothing. I heard nothing except my own voice. I constantly pushed my doubts back into my subconscious mind. *Concentrate Mustafa, concentrate. Your brother needs you now.*

I finally looked down at my watch. It was about 4:00 a.m., and the people would be coming for dawn prayer in about an hour. I had to get ready for them because the building still had no electricity. I gathered as many candles as I could and put them in the windows of the mosque. I also found two large iron lanterns and put them at the front door. Then I hurried back to our home.

I tapped on the door of Sheikh Ahmed's room. "Hello. Are you there?" I said, hoping that he changed his mind and decided to stay with us. There was no reply. I knocked louder. Still no answer. Finally, I pushed the door open and found the room empty, the bed still neatly made as it had been the morning before. He'd never slept there. Even though he said he would be gone, I felt the disappointment deep in my gut, like a physical pain.

I called my father's cell phone, and he answered in a hoarse voice. "How is Sayid?" I asked.

He paused. "Sayid is in a coma. The doctors don't know what is going to happen. Your mother is taking this very hard. She hasn't stopped crying since we got here."

"My father," I said, "I'm going to do dawn prayers at the mosque right now, and then I'm coming to see you. I've been praying all night."

"Bring your friend the sheikh," my dad said, "so that he can pray too."

"I'll be there soon, Father," I said again. I couldn't bring myself to tell him that Sheikh Ahmed had left.

[*Chapter 22*]

The Angel of Death Speaks

The neighborhood had already heard about Sayid, and at dawn prayers there were tear-stained faces all over the mosque. I led the prayers, and then my older brother and I ran to my car and raced through the empty streets to the hospital.

My heart sank when we walked into the room. My brother's face was gray and sunken. He had oxygen tubes in his nose and IVs in his arm. My father stood at the head of the bed, gently stroking his face and hair with his hand. My father didn't look up when we walked in. My mother sat crumpled in a chair at the foot of the bed, sobbing weakly. "There's nothing they can do," she choked out the words as the tears flowed. Then she asked, "Where is Sheikh Ahmed? Why hasn't he come to pray with us?"

"My mother, I'm so sorry," I answered. "He had to leave." We stayed there as the sun rose higher in the sky—praying and waiting and hoping. By noon Sayid's breaths were slower and shallower. He fought for every breath, his face tense, his mouth gaping open. I desperately wanted to take the breaths from my lungs and give them to my brother.

Sayid was facing the moment of his life that every Muslim dreads the most. According to Muhammad's teaching, as the last breaths are drawn, the dying person sees the terrifying image of the angel of death looming over him, ready to take his soul. This angel has no words of comfort. He proclaims, "O slave of Allah, the disease and pain were nothing but the last meal before death. How many meals did you receive during your life? I am the meal that no meal comes after. I walked around the world in the east and the west looking for another piece of bread for you to eat, and I could not find it. I walked around the world looking for another breath for you to breathe, and I could not find it. Answer your Lord: Do you like it or not? This is the day of your death."

As my brother struggled, I imagined the angel of death, pulling the spirit out of his body. If Allah decided my brother lived a good enough life, then the spirit would come out easily, like water pouring out of a pitcher. But if Allah judged that my brother did not fulfill his duties well enough, then the angel would rip the spirit out of his body, starting from his feet, through the legs, to his stomach and chest, and finally pulling the spirit out of his mouth, causing indescribable pain. This is why we dreaded and feared the moment of Sayid's death. Allah did not reveal any way for us to know for sure that the angel would take Sayid's spirit gently.

At that instant, as I stood next to Sayid's bed, I felt a distinct emotion: I was furious. I was not furious because Sayid was dying. I was sad about his dying, but I understood his death was the result of physical, human frailty. I did not blame Allah for his death or for not healing him. I was furious because I—even though I was a faithful Muslim—could not have spiritual peace at the time of Sayid's death. Every death of someone I loved would be a time of agonizing uncertainty. And I dreaded my own death as well.

Islam says the angel of death will speak again when he hears the cries of those gathered around their dying loved one. He speaks with a voice that can be heard by animals and by the rest of creation, but not by any human being:

> For whom do you cry? Why do you cry? I swear in Allah, I did not save a provision to keep him alive, and I didn't take one day away from his life. Allah called him, and he has to answer to Allah whether he likes it or not. You who are crying, cry for yourselves, because I will be back

again and again and again until I take all of you.

I wanted to scream at Allah, "Why would you send an angel to taunt us? Where is your love? Where is your mercy?"

I never took my eyes off Sayid's face, hoping for a sign that he was at peace. But his last breath was just like all the ones that preceded it. No better, no worse. Sayid was dead. His eyes were open, staring at the ceiling, as if he had seen the angel of death carrying his soul away. When my mother realized he had stopped breathing, she immediately began to sob hysterically, burying her face in her heavy black burqa so that her cries would not be too loud.

With his hands trembling, my father gently closed Sayid's eyelids as he choked out the pronouncement of death: "From Allah we come and to Allah we return." My father's body heaved as he sobbed silently, and my brother and I wept with him. We clung to Sayid's lifeless body, not wanting to let him go.

We could not grieve together for long. Within an hour, one of my mother's brothers picked her up and took her back to our house. The hospital brought the death certificate so that we could bury Sayid before sunset that day, just as the Prophet had taught. Uncle Hamzi, my father's brother, arrived quickly to help us with the burial preparations. I felt weak as I helped my older brother lift Sayid's body so my father and uncle could wrap him in a new white sheet. Before my father covered Sayid's face for the last time, I kissed his eyes and his cheeks.

We did not take Sayid's body to a funeral home, because in the Muslim community, the family cares for the bodies of their loved ones. My brother and I lifted Sayid's body onto a heavy, white tarp, and then the four of us took hold of the corners and carried the body out of the hospital to my father's car. We gently laid the limp form into the back seat. "I'll sit back here," I said, "to make sure the body doesn't slide." I wanted to be as close to Sayid as I could, even for a few more minutes.

As my father drove to our home I looked at Sayid's body and wondered, *Are you in pain, my dear brother? What did Allah decide to do to you?* At home, we laid his body on his bed in his room. If his face had been uncovered, it would have looked like he was just sleeping.

The word of Sayid's death had gone out to our relatives and neighbors. When we arrived at our house, my mother was already surrounded by women dressed in black, weeping with her as she sat in the living room. Our relatives and friends were coming together to prepare for the burial. The house was alive with people coming and going and asking questions.

I went to my room and sat on the bed. I could hear all the commotion in the house, but I needed to be alone.

"Hold open the door," I heard a neighbor call out, as family members carried in the casket from our neighborhood mosque and put it in the living room.

"The funeral prayer is at 6:00 p.m.," one of my aunts announced to everyone who came in the door. Every time I heard a knock at the door, deep inside I hoped that it was Sheikh Ahmed.

I wondered, *If he really is the Prophet, would he know that Sayid has died? Will he come to comfort us and help us intercede to Allah for Sayid's forgiveness?*

I felt the cell phone in my pocket, and for the first time since he gave it to me, I looked at it closely. It looked like a normal cell phone, but there were some scratches on it from when I fainted. The digital numbers on the front showed the correct time, and the battery was fully charged. *How would I call him?* I wondered. He didn't give me a phone number. I flipped open the phone to look at the keypad. The display screen held a message: "To place a call, press and hold 1."

Well, at least he answered that question, I thought with a feeling of bitterness. I folded the phone shut. *Should I call him now? Should I ask him to pray with us for Allah to have mercy on my brother?*

I heard my father calling my name. "Mustafa," he said, "it is time. We need to do the washing." Quickly I shoved the phone back in my pocket.

Chapter 23

Pray for Mercy

When I entered Sayid's room, I saw that my father and uncle had prepared everything for the washing. Sayid's body, still covered with a white sheet, was on a tall washing table that my family borrowed from the mosque. Underneath it was a large, shallow basin for catching the water. Four of my mother's biggest cooking pots sat on the floor next to the table, filled to the brim with warm water. On Sayid's dresser I saw more supplies we would need for the washing: a pitcher, a bar of soap, a small cloth, clean towels, and a spray bottle.

My older brother was standing with my father and uncle, and a quiet, bearded man wearing a dark gray robe was sitting in a chair. He was the *hanuti*, a representative from the mosque specially trained in the burial rituals.

We heard a soft knock on the door, and my sister, Hoda, said through the door, "The shrouds are here." My sister had been in charge of getting the shrouds made. The moment she heard Sayid had died, she quickly purchased fabric and took it to the seamstress who made burial shrouds. They were very simple—just two large rectangles of fabric sewn together with an opening at the top. The body would go inside the shroud completely. The first shroud was pure white. The second shroud was made out of a rich, shimmering beige fabric.

My uncle looked at me solemnly. "Mustafa," he said, "we know you and Sayid were as close as brothers can be. Your father and I agree that you should have the honor of leading the washing." I could see the tears in my father's eyes.

"Thank you," I answered hoarsely, feeling a wave of gratitude. I picked up the soap and cloth and the *hanuti* joined me with the pitcher. "There is no God but Allah," I said and removed the sheet so that I could wash Sayid's body. When I saw his face, I felt like I could hardly breathe. *How could he be gone so quickly? I would miss his smile and his laughter so much.*

Men in our culture try to control their emotions, but I could see the tears on their faces as my father, uncle, and brother helped me to turn Sayid's body on its left side. The *hanuti* dipped the pitcher into one of the pots of water and poured a thin stream onto Sayid's head. I followed with the soapy washcloth.

"Sayid," I said as I wiped his face, "I am so sad that you have departed, but I will not be selfish about missing you because you are going to a better place, and you will be full of joy." The words sounded hollow as I spoke them. I loved Sayid with all my heart, but I didn't know if Allah would punish him or comfort him. I felt full of despair.

With great effort, I kept my emotions under control. I could hear the women crying and mourning in the living room. I felt numb as I washed the right side of Sayid's body with a soapy washcloth. Then we turned his body and washed the left side. We were silent except when my uncle occasionally quoted from the Quran.

We washed him three times this way and then it was time to scent his body. My brother handed me the spray bottle, and soon the strong, sharp smell of camphor filled the room as I sprayed it over Sayid's body. This was the smell of death.

The ritual was almost finished. Together we lifted Sayid's body and covered him in the white shroud and sprayed the camphor over it. Then we lifted him again and pulled the outer shroud on top. My father reluctantly tied the silken cords, closing the ends of the shrouds. We would never see my brother's face again.

As we opened the door of the room, the muffled sound of the women weeping became loud and strong. We carried Sayid's body on the white tarp through the house to the living room. My mother and sister Hoda were waiting there next to the casket, surrounded by female relatives and friends. Hoda held my mother close as we placed Sayid's body in the casket.

It was time to take Sayid for his final visit to the mosque. My father and uncle grasped the two handles on the front of the casket, and my brother and I took the ones in the back and we carried the casket out of the living room, out of the house, and into the street with dozens of relatives and neighbors following us. The men followed directly behind the casket, while the women, including my mother and sister, walked together in a group at the back of the procession. While we were still several blocks from the mosque, we could see the gathering crowd.

My family was large and well-known in the area. Throngs of people filled the mosque and spilled outside—probably a thousand people altogether. The women stood in a group outside the mosque while we carried the casket into the mosque, and the men followed us inside. The women would wait outside the mosque during the funeral prayer. We walked slowly through the crowded mosque and placed the casket at the front on the right-hand side. Less than twenty-four hours earlier I had paced through this mosque all night, praying for Sayid to live. Now I would stand with a thousand people to say the prayers of death.

Uncle Hamzi led the prayer with his deep, melodic voice. "*Allahu Akbar*," he called out, and with one voice we replied, "*Allahu Akbar*." He led us through the general prayers and then he prayed: "O Allah, forgive those of us that are alive and those of us that are dead; those of us that are present, and those of us who are absent: those of us that are young, and those of us that are adults; our males and females. O Allah! Whomsoever of us you keep alive, let him live as a follower of Islam, and whomsoever you cause to die, let him die as a believer."

That's exactly the prayer that Muhammad said in the seventh century, I thought to myself, *but I'm not sure it will make any difference with Allah. The Quran says there will be no intercession on the Day of Judgment (2:254), but the hadith says that Muhammad can intercede for us. Why are there so many contradictions in Islam? What are we supposed to believe?* Tears poured down my face as the funeral prayers ended—tears of frustration and sorrow.

After the funeral prayer, my father, uncle, brother, and I picked up the casket again and carried it out of the mosque and down the road toward the cemetery, just as they did in the seventh century. The men followed us, but my mother and the other women went back to our house to continue mourning.

It was a four-mile walk to the cemetery on the other side of the Nile River. My head throbbed and my left knee ached from my fall that morning as we climbed the bridge over the Nile. I thought about what Sayid was experiencing. Muhammad said a dead person will cry out as he is being carried to his grave. If he lived a good life, he will cry, "Hurry, hurry, hurry," because he sees that his grave has become a piece of Paradise and he will want to go quickly. But if the person did evil, he will cry out, "Slow down, slow down, slow down," because he sees that his grave has become a little hell, a place of torture. In his grave, two angels with iron hammers will beat him between his ears.

The torture of the grave puts fear of death in the heart of every Muslim. As we carried Sayid's coffin through the streets, I thought with frustration, *If Allah is a God of mercy, why does he torment us with this fear of the grave?*

We reached the cemetery, and the men gathered around the sloping passageway that led to the small underground room that was my family's tomb. The body of my grandfather had been laid on the floor there two years earlier. We lifted my brother's body from the casket and laid it next to my grandfather's body, wrapped in its shrouds.

Again we prayed for Allah's mercy on Sayid, and my father's last duty was to push a little berm of sand around Sayid's body where it lay on the floor of the tomb. After the burial, my father looked exhausted. "Father," I said, "let's ask some of our cousins to take the casket back to the mosque." Already, hands were reaching out to take it.

"Thank you," he said hoarsely. We followed the throng of men walking out of the cemetery. We did not return home. That was the place for my mother and sister and their friends. They would mourn together for the next three days, removing their head covers and scooping dust onto their hair with their hands.

I walked with the men back over the bridge over the Nile River to the large meeting hall that my grandfather had built near the mosque for family gatherings. Because we were one of the biggest families in the area, our hall could hold up to three hundred people.

As we approached the hall I heard a familiar sound: it was the voice of a Quran reciter. Muhammad once said, "When you have a funeral for one who has died, recite the Quran because the Quran is going to be his intercessor." In other words, Muhammad said that speaking the words of the Quran would be a way to beseech Allah to show favor to the one who has died. So when a Muslim dies, his family will make sure the Quran is recited as much as possible. Some families even hire a man to recite the Quran at the gravesite.

"I hired two reciters, Mustafa," my uncle said. "They will take turns and make sure the Quran is being recited from 6:00 in the morning until 2:00 at night. May Allah have mercy on us."

I looked at the reciter, with his eyes closed and his hand gripping the microphone. A little cup of water was next to him. I felt frustration rising up inside me. *We are pouring water into a bucket full of holes. How can we ever reach the top?*

I was so exhausted. I had not slept in almost thirty-six hours. As soon as I found a chair to sit in, I fell asleep. In my dreams, I was walking through the dark mosque again, crying to Allah to have mercy on Sayid.

[Chapter 24]

Judgment Day

The three days of mourning were a blur. Groups of families came to the hall bringing meals for us to eat. All the people who came to mourn with us also prayed in our little neighborhood mosque, which made it much busier than usual. Many extra prayers were made on Sayid's behalf.

When one of the reciters felt weak, I filled in for him for a couple of hours. I felt as if I were trying to fill a bucket with holes in the bottom. *How many verses does it take to please Allah? How many words need to pour out of our mouths?"*

We slept on the couches at night.

Once my father asked me, "Did you tell your friend Sheikh Ahmed what has happened?"

"He knows," I answered.

"Why hasn't he come?" my dad asked.

"I think he had to go far away on business," I answered, hoping my dad would believe me. "He is a much busier person than I first realized."

To my relief, a distant cousin arrived to greet my father, so the conversation ended.

Every once in a while I would check my pocket to make sure I still had the cell phone. *I could call Sheikh Ahmed,* I thought, *but I have nothing to say.*

The next Monday, I went back to Al-Azhar to teach classes. All through the day, students and other lecturers would say to me, "Dr. Rahal, I said a prayer for your brother," or, "May Allah have mercy on your family." Dr. Abdu's eyes filled with tears when he saw me.

As I went through the day, I had this strange sensation of being disconnected from what I was doing. It was as if I were watching myself in a movie. There I was, washing for prayer. There I was praying at the mosque. There I was teaching class. There I was walking back to my car to go home.

That day, my mother had prepared my brother's favorite meal—Egyptian fish with rice and salad. When I came home, the table was heaping with food, and my mother was washing dishes in the kitchen, dressed completely in black, her eyes red from weeping. "Mother," I said, "dinner looks wonderful. Thank you."

She nodded.

"Mother," I said, trying to comfort her, "everyone at the university told me today how they are praying for Allah to have mercy on Sayid. Allah will hear our prayers."

She began to sob, and I felt tears in my own eyes. "It's OK," I said weakly. "It's OK." I was lying. Everything wasn't OK.

When my father came home, we tried to eat the food my mother had prepared. It stuck in my throat, and I could hardly swallow, but I tried to enjoy it for her sake. As soon as we were finished, I told my parents, "I'm going to the mosque early for the sunset prayers. I need to think."

I kept Sheikh Ahmed's cell phone in my pocket at all times, and

I never told anyone about our final conversation—partly because I was afraid of what would happen if I broke my promise to him and partly because I didn't think anyone would believe me anyway. Regardless of his identity, Sheikh Ahmed was right about my faith; I was at a crossroads, and I had not decided which way to walk.

When I arrived, the mosque was nearly empty. I found a place where I could be alone, sat down on the floor, and closed my eyes. I knew people would think I was reciting the Quran.

I thought about Sayid. He had gone to the grave before me, but the Quran said I would see him on Resurrection Day, when a trumpet blast sounds and every man, woman, and child who ever lived will come out of their graves to stand before Allah in the Judgment Square (Surah 27:87).

There Sayid and I would face Allah and his scales. Allah would put Sayid's good deeds on one side and his bad deeds on the other (Surah 99:7–8). I imagined there would be a horrible moment when Allah released the scales and they swung back and forth. Would it be close for Sayid? Would there be just enough good for him to go to Paradise? If so, then Allah would say to him, "Peace," and Sayid would enter into the garden and sit on a cushioned throne in the shade where he would eat fruit in abundance and drink from rivers of milk, honey, and alcohol. He would have beautiful women to enjoy and children to serve him.

If the bad deeds were heavier, even by one atom, Allah would say to Sayid, "Do you receive a reward other than that which you have earned by your deeds?" And Sayid would be thrown face first into the fire (Surah 27:90). As soon as the skin burned off his body, a fresh skin would appear so that his torture would never end (Surah 4:56). At the same time, he would be given a boiling, festering liquid to drink (Surah 14:16–17).

As he was tortured in hell, Sayid and the other inhabitants of hell would cry out to the angel Malek, the keeper of hell, "O Malek, ask your Allah to destroy us." After hearing their cry for one thousand years, Malek would answer the people, "You will be here forever. Allah judged the people and you have been judged already" (Surah 43:77).

My heart was breaking as I thought of this picture. I mourned for Sayid, but I also mourned for myself and for every Muslim. None of us could know how Allah would judge. If I called Sheikh Ahmed and asked him, "Will you go to Paradise on Judgment Day?" he would say, "I do not know," just as Muhammad said in the seventh century.

I thought bitterly, *The Prophet revealed every detail about the pleasures of heaven, the tortures of hell, the regulations of prayer, the rituals of the* hajj, *and the daily duties of Muslim life. There were volumes and volumes of books about these things. But when it came to the life after death, he only gave one way to be sure that a person would go to Paradise, which was to die in jihad. But if you died any other way, then all you could do was hope. This meant a life of inner turmoil and terror for every Muslim. No wonder Muslim radicals are the source of most of the world terrorism. They are spreading the terror that is already rooted in their psyches by the teachings of Islam. Was this the life I wanted? Was this the nature of the true God of heaven?*

I struggled with my emotions. If Sayid lived, would I still be questioning Islam? Maybe not as much, I had to admit. Or maybe not right now. But the questions would still be the same. Sayid's death did not change the questions that I struggled with. I opened my eyes. As I had been thinking, the mosque filled up with the faithful who had come for the sunset prayer. My body had become part of a row of men who came to do their duty before Allah.

As we prayed, the familiar words flowed like water over my tongue, and I imagined a stream flowing from each person's mouth and flooding the mosque as we prayed, only to flow out the doors and sink into the sand without a trace.

I stayed at the mosque for the sunset and night prayer, and then I walked home around 9:30 p.m. I was exhausted and wanted to sleep, but since Sayid's death, I would lie awake in my bed for hours. That night, I gave up on sleeping, and I went up on the rooftop instead to look at the stars. I sat in the same chair where I sat the night Sheikh Ahmed gave me the cell phone.

I tried to think logically about whether Sheikh Ahmed could really be the Prophet. He spoke like the Prophet. He acted like the Prophet. He knew things about my life that almost no one else knew.

Let's say he really was the Prophet, I thought to myself. *What did I learn that I didn't already know? Everything he did confirmed what I already knew from the Quran and the hadith.*

Now, I thought, *what if the opposite were true. Let's say that Sheikh Ahmed was not the Prophet. He was just a crazy Saudi tribesman. What would that change? The answer is* nothing. *The nature and character of the apostle of Allah remain the same.*

Finally, a clear thought broke into my mind: *What really matters is whether Muhammad spoke for the true God of heaven.*

This idea was like a lantern shining in a dark room.

My thoughts tumbled on top of one another. Yes, that's it! I know what Muhammad said and did, but what I need to know is, Did the true God of heaven speak to him? Did the true God of heaven give him Islam, or did Muhammad invent it? Is Islam the path to righteousness or a dead end? Did Muhammad express the heart of the true, merciful God, or did he merely express the dark corners of his own faulty human heart?

The implication shook me to the core: If the true God never spoke to Muhammad, then I am a slave to the manipulative imagination of a desert tribesman from the seventh century!

These were dangerous thoughts, and I had crossed a dangerous bridge in my mind that all Muslims are taught to walk away from. If I valued my life, I would turn around and go back. But I couldn't. If I didn't cross that bridge, I would throw myself in the water and drown.

I put my hand in my pocket and felt the cell phone. It was time.

I stood up and walked down the stairs of the house and out the front door. I walked down the road we took when we carried Sayid's coffin to the cemetery until I was standing in the middle of the bridge over the Nile River. I looked over the railing for a moment. The water sparkled with the reflection of the lights on its banks. I pulled the cell phone out of my pocket and flipped it open. The instructions on the screen remained the same: "To place a call, press and hold 1." I noticed the battery was still fully charged. I could call Sheikh Ahmed any time I wanted, but I had nothing more to discuss with him.

With one motion, I snapped the phone shut, drew my hand behind my head, and flung the phone as hard and as far as I could. I could just barely see the splash in the rippling waters.

I held my breath for a minute and looked around me, wondering if Allah would strike me dead for my insolence. Nothing happened. Maybe only the Nile River knew what I had done. I turned and walked off the other end of the bridge. I didn't know where I was going, but it would not be where I had been.

What Happened to Mustafa?

A Word from Dr. Mark A. Gabriel

Where Mustafa's story ends, my story begins. When I finished my doctorate at Al-Azhar, I was like Mustafa, struggling with my faith. I began to defy Al-Azhar norms and critique Islamic history with my students until a committee of professors called me to a meeting to explain my actions. That's when I crossed the bridge, metaphorically speaking, just as Mustafa did. I told the professors, "Listen, I need your help. We say the Quran is directly from Allah, but I doubt it. I see in it the thoughts of a man, not the words of a true God."

There was no turning back from a statement like that. One professor spit in my face. "You blasphemer," he snarled, "get out!"

I left campus and drove home to my parent's house where I lived with my father, mother, brothers, and sisters. I knew something would happen to me, but I didn't know what. That night secret police with machine guns kidnapped me from my bed, and threw me in a prison cell. The guards began torturing me the next day. They were convinced that I had converted to Christianity, and they demanded: "What pastor did you talk to? What church have you been visiting? Why did you betray Islam?"

I told them defiantly, "I haven't done anything wrong, and I haven't converted to Christianity. I was only asking questions, which is my right as a human being."

I was not yet an apostate, but the laws of apostasy had been set in motion against me. I did not think I would get out of the prison alive. However, after a week, the guards stopped the torture, and for reasons I never learned, I was transferred to a permanent prison and the interrogations were stopped.

All this time, my family could not even find out where I was. Finally, through a relative with a government position, they located me and secured my release. When I came out alive, I was looking for the God who saved my life, but I was convinced that Islam was not the way to reach him.

After a year of searching for the path to the true God of heaven, I was depressed and sick. I experienced splitting headaches and took pain medication regularly. One day when I was getting my medication from the pharmacist, she sent me home with more than just pills. It was a black leather-bound book I had never read before.

Between its covers I met the Prophet who showed me the path that I sought. This Prophet led me to the true God of heaven and showed me that God loved me. Instead of threatening me with judgment, this Prophet went to judgment in my place and sacrificed his own body on the scales so that I would not live in fear about life after death. This Prophet made a promise that rings in my ears every day: "I will never leave you or forsake you."

Today, I walk with this Prophet, and my soul is at peace.

Notes

The Research Supporting Coffee with the Prophet

This book tells a fictional story focused on two fictional characters: Dr. Mustafa al-Rahal and Sheikh Ahmed. However, many of the events and details in the book are based on fact. In other words, when you read something about Sheikh Ahmed, there is a good chance that it was derived from the life of Muhammad. Also, when you read about Mustafa, there is a good chance it is something I experienced personally.

The Notes section of this book will give you deeper insight into the research and facts that make up the foundation of this story. It is organized by chapter and can be used as a reference tool or it can be read in its entirety. Sources will list whether they are in English or Arabic. I have also compiled a glossary to help you with terms that may be unfamiliar to you.

All names included in this story, with the exception of public figures such as Dr. Ezzat Atiyah or Dr. Naguib Mahfouz, are fictitious. The fictitious names do not correspond to my family's names or the names of other people I have known. If there is a resemblance between these fictitious names and names of actual people, it is unintentional.

In addition, I want to be clear that Mustafa's family is fictional. Mustafa's family is similar to my own family but does not have the same number of siblings or the same names.

The Cover Art

The image that appears on the cover of *Coffee with the Prophet* is based on extensive research into the descriptions of Muhammad supplied by his wives and companions. These descriptions were given to a professional artist who produced the picture. The result is a respectful image that gives readers a realistic idea of what Muhammad looked like. This picture can in no way be deemed an insult because it is true to the descriptions in the hadith. Here is an overview of the resources that were used:

General appearance

> The Prophet was neither conspicuously tall, nor short; neither very white, nor tawny. His hair was neither much curled, nor very straight. Allah sent him (as an Apostle) at the age of forty (and after that) he stayed for ten years in Mecca, and for ten more years in Medina. Allah took him unto Him at the age of sixty, and he scarcely had ten white hairs on his head and in his beard.[1]

> The Prophet had big feet and a good-looking face and I have not seen anybody like him after him. Narrated Anas: The Prophet had big feet and hands. Narrated Anas or Jabir bin 'Abdullah: The Prophet had big hands and feet and I have not seen anybody like him after him.[2]

> The Apostle of Allah, may Allah bless him, is neither too short nor too tall. His hairs are neither curly nor straight,

[1] Narrated Anas bin Malik in *The Correct Books of Bukhari* (in English), vol. 7, bk. 72, no. 787, http://www.usc.edu/dept/MSA/fundamentals/hadithsunnah/bukhari/072.sbt.html#007.072.787 (accessed September 2008).

[2] Narrated Abu Huraira in *The Correct Books of Bukhari* (in English), vol. 7, bk. 72, no. 794, http://www.usc.edu/dept/MSA/fundamentals/hadithsunnah/bukhari/072.sbt.html#007.072.794 (accessed September 2008).

> but a mixture of the two. He is a man of black hair and large skull. His complexion has a tinge of redness. His shoulder bones are broad and his palms and feet are fleshy. He has long al-masrubah which means hair growing from neck to navel. He is of long eye-lashes, close eye-brows, smooth and shining fore-head and long space between two shoulders. When he walks he walks inclining as if coming down from a height. I never saw a man like him before him or after him.[3]

Hair

> I asked Anas bin Malik about the hair of Allah's Apostle. He said, "The hair of Allah's Apostle was neither much straight, nor much curly, and it used to hang down till between his shoulders and his earlobes."[4]

Sandals

> The sandal of the Prophet had two straps.[5]

Silver ring

> Allah's Apostle took a silver ring and had "Muhammad, the Apostle of Allah" engraved on it. The Prophet then said (to us), "I have a silver ring with 'Muhammad, the Apostle of Allah' engraved on it, so none of you should have the same engraving on his ring."[6]

---

[3] Ibn Sa'd, *Kitabh al-Tabaqat al-Kabir* [*The Highest Level*], as translated by S. Moinul and H.K. Ghazanfar (New Delhi: Kitab Bhavan, n.d.).

[4] Narrated Qatada in *The Correct Books of Bukhari* (in English), vol. 7, bk. 72, no. 791, http://www.usc.edu/dept/MSA/fundamentals/hadithsunnah/bukhari/072.sbt.html#007.072.791 (accessed September 2008).

[5] Narrated Anas in *The Correct Books of Bukhari* (in English), vol. 7, bk. 72, no. 748, http://www.usc.edu/dept/MSA/fundamentals/hadithsunnah/bukhari/072.sbt.html#007.072.748 (accessed September 2008).

[6] Narrated Anas bin Malik in *The Correct Books of Bukhari* (in English), vol. 7, bk. 72, no. 766, http://www.usc.edu/dept/MSA/fundamentals/hadithsunnah/bukhari/072.sbt.html#007.072.766 (accessed September 2008).

Turban

> Jabir b. Abdullah reported that Allah's Apostle (may peace be upon him) entered on the day of Victory of Mecca wearing a black turban on his head.[7]

The Controversy About Making Images of the Prophet

The Muslim response to the Danish cartoons was shocking. Hundreds of thousands of people rioted. Products from Denmark were boycotted. Danish embassies were attacked and Danish flags burned. What caused this kind of outrage?[8]

The Western media usually blame the violent response on "Islam's prohibition of any artistic depiction of the prophet Muhammad, which is considered blasphemous, no matter how benign."[9]

This explanation begs the question: Were the Danish cartoons the first images ever made of the Prophet Muhammad? Of course not. Did all the previous images of the Prophet spark this kind of outrage? No. So what is really going on here?

The answer to this question has two parts. First, what does Islam say about making an image of the Prophet? Second, what does Islam say about insulting the Prophet, because there is where the heart of the matter lies. The Muslim world did not protest an image; they protested an *insulting* image.

Making Images of the Prophet

First of all, it is important to understand that no place in the Quran or the hadith prohibits making an image of the Prophet in particular. The ban is for depictions of any living thing (i.e., animals

---

[7] *The Correct Books of Muslim* (in English), bk. 7, no. 3147, http://www.usc.edu/dept/MSA/fundamentals/hadithsunnah/muslim/007.smt.html#007.3147 (accessed September 2008).

[8] John Ward Anderson, "Cartoons of Prophet Met With Outrage," Washington Post Foreign Service, January 31, 2006, http://www.washingtonpost.com/wp-dyn/content/article/2006/01/30/AR2006013001316.html (accessed September 2008).

[9] Ibid.

or people). And not all Muslims accept this ban.

First, let's look at the Quranic evidence. The Quran forbids images that are used for idol worship, but not representational art in general.

> Behold! he said to his father and his people, "What are these *images*, to which ye are (so assiduously) devoted?" They said, "We found our fathers worshipping them." He said, "Indeed ye have been in manifest error—ye and your fathers" (Surah 21:52–54, Ali, italics added).

However, in some hadith Muhammad says that any picture of a living thing (a person or animal) is prohibited. By extension, a picture of Muhammad would be prohibited as well. The hadith commonly quoted are:

> I heard him say: All the painters who make pictures would be in the fire of Hell. The soul will be breathed in every picture prepared by him and it shall punish him in the Hell, and he (Ibn 'Abbas) said: If you have to do it at all, then paint the pictures of trees and lifeless things; and Nasr b. 'Ali confirmed it.[10]

> Allah, Most High said: "And who is more unjust than those who try to create the likeness of My creation? Let them create an atom, or let them create a wheat grain, or let them create a barley grain."[11]

There is a big difference between Sunni and Shia regarding making a picture of Muhammad. The Shia have generally allowed images of the Prophet because they reject the hadith narrated by

---

[10] *The Correct Books of Muslim* (in English), bk. 24, no. 5272, http://www.usc.edu/dept/MSA/fundamentals/hadithsunnah/muslim/024.smt.html#024.5272 (accessed September 2008).

[11] *The Correct Books of Bukhari* (in English), vol. 9, bk. 93, no. 648, http://www.usc.edu/dept/MSA/fundamentals/hadithsunnah/bukhari/093.sbt.html#009.093.648 (accessed September 2008).

Aisha, and Aisha narrated the main hadith about not making pictures. On the other hand, Sunni accept Aisha's hadith and usually reject making pictures of people or animals. The medieval scholar Ibn Taymiyyah and his disciples Ibn Kayim and Ibn Kathir revived the prohibition against pictures of living things.

Having said that, you can go to the website http://www.zombietime.com/mohammed_image_archive/ and view an extensive collection of art featuring Muhammad. This site was established in response to the cartoon controversy. The home page explains: "The inspiration for this archive came from the global controversy over the publication of Mohammed cartoons in the Danish newspaper *Jyllands-Posten*, and the need for a comprehensive and even-handed look at the wide variety of Mohammed depictions in Islamic and Western societies from the Middle Ages until today. It will remain online as a resource for those interested in freedom of expression."

This site notes that "several books about Islam (mostly published in Europe within the last 20 years) have unabashedly depicted Mohammed on their covers. None of the book covers shown here caused any uproar in the Muslim world." These book covers can also be viewed on the website.

Insulting the Prophet

Now let's look at the second question: what does Islam say about insulting the Prophet? The Muslim world did not protest an image; they protested an *insulting* image. Insulting the Prophet can be interpreted broadly to mean saying something against the religion, or against Muhammad's lineage, or saying that Muhammad or the religion is impure. The famous scholar Ibn Taymiyyah says that no one should even say the Prophet's clothes are dirty because that is like saying he is impure.

Muhammad did not tolerate insults if he was able to silence them. He ordered assassinations if necessary. Here is a good example, taken from my book, *Journey into the Mind of an Islamic Terrorist*:

> Muhammad asked a group of his friends, "Who will take care of Kaab bin Ashraf for me?" (Kaab had been writing poetry that criticized the Prophet.)
>
> A man named Muhammad bin Musslemah said, "Would you like me to kill him?"
>
> Muhammad responded, "Yes."
>
> Musslemah answered, "Permit me to say things [meaning to lie]."
>
> Muhammad gave him permission.
>
> Musslemah went to the poet and pretended to be displeased with Muhammad and in need of a loan. He convinced the poet to allow him to secure the loan with weapons and promised to return the following night.
>
> So Musslemah came back the next night with two men [and the weapons] and went out for a walk with the poet. As the poet and Musslemah walked, Musslemah held him by the hair as if to kiss [greet] him and held him while the other two men ambushed him and cut off his head.
>
> Muhammad justified the assassination by saying: "If he [the poet] had stayed silent just as everyone who shared his same opinion stayed, he wouldn't have been murdered. But he harmed us with his poetry, and any one of you who did that would have deserved the sword."[12]

So the violent reaction in the Muslim world was mainly rooted in defending the Prophet against insult rather than defending the Prophet against being drawn.

Dedication

I was one of a group of college professors, intellectual people, and writers who regularly met with Dr. Mahfouz in the 1990s at the Rish Coffee Shop. He paid extra attention to those of us from Al-Azhar because he saw Muslim scholars as the hope for the Islamic world. He believed that more freedom in the religious community would

---

[12] Mark Gabriel, *Journey Into the Mind of an Islamic Terrorist* (Lake Mary, Fla.: Charisma House, 2007), p. 121. See also Ibn Ishaq, *The Biography of the Prophet* (in English), p. 364ff.

mean more freedom in society as a whole.

In 1994, at the age of eighty-two, he was stabbed in the neck by a Muslim radical who was angry at his portrayal of God in one of his novels. The attack caused nerve damage in his neck and deterioration to his eyesight and hearing. The last thing he published was a 2005 collection of stories about the afterlife titled *The Seventh Heaven.* He died on August 30, 2006, at the age of ninety-four.[13]

Acknowledgements

My deepest appreciation to a dear friend, who believed in this project, encouraged me to see it through and helped make it all possible. I also thank my writing collaborator who helped me created the fiction story line.

Chapter 1: I Am a *Hafiz*

Mustafa in this story is a reflection of the person I was a little less than twenty years ago. I also completed memorizing the Quran by the time I was twelve years old, and Mustafa's education exactly mirrors my own. The main difference is that I went to *hajj* twice in reality—in 1987 and 1991. The first time, in 1987, I took my grandfather on the pilgrimage before he died, and the second time, in 1991, I went on the *hajj* as a guest of the Islamic University of Medina, where I was a guest lecturer for a few months.

I want to make one clarification regarding *hajj* dates. The two times that I did the *hajj* personally were in August and June, so I experienced the full heat of summer in Saudi Arabia. In this fictional story, Mustafa does the pilgrimage in August 2008, even though the *hajj* dates for 2008 are in the beginning of December. However, I chose to have Mustafa in the story experience a summer *hajj* as I did.

The incident where Mustafa challenged the professor about jihad

---

13 "President Pays Tribute to Mahfouz, BBC News, August 30, 2006, http://news.bbc.co.uk/2/hi/middle_east/5297470.stm (accessed October 2008).

came from my own life. The professor I challenged was Sheikh Omar Abdul Rahman, the blind sheikh who masterminded the 1993 bombing of the underground garage of the World Trade Centers. In his answer to me, Abdul Rahman was quoting Muhammad's words when he said, "Jihad is the head of Islam."[14]

Chapter 2: The Holy Ground

In this chapter, Mustafa experiences the Day of Standing, the most holy day of the *hajj.* Like Mustafa, I also climbed as high as I could on Mount Arafat when I went on my second *hajj*, and I was disturbed deeply by the yawning silence in between the chanting of the people. I felt the silence of heaven.

During much of the *hajj*, pilgrims camp in the huge tent cities established by the Saudi government.

Chapter 3: Family Secret

It is often said that truth is stranger than fiction. This part of Mustafa's story is almost entirely based on my own childhood, with a few minor changes to fit the story line. As a twelve-year-old in the early 1960s, I did attack a Christian priest, but not by throwing rocks at his house. I sabotaged his donkey's saddle with a homemade firecracker. When the firecracker exploded, the donkey bucked the priest off and the priest was seriously injured. My father was furious and beat me for the first time in my life. Another time, I led the Muslim kids on a raid to the Christian neighborhood where we threw stones at houses and broke windows. So Mustafa's story is a combination of these events.

This chapter also includes a scene where Mustafa's mother takes him to bake bread and reveals that he was nursed by a Christian woman when he was a baby. The family feared that his faith in Islam would be corrupted by this experience, so they immersed him in the study of Islam. This is exactly what happened in my life.

---

[14] *Sahih Tirmizi*

Chapter 4: Stoning Satan

I went through all the rituals of the *hajj* just as I described them. The *tawaf*, or walking around al-Ka'aba, really did cause me to question the logic of what I was doing. As I was walking, I thought about Umar saying to the stone, "If I didn't see the Prophet do this, I would never do it."[15]

In addition to the duties of *hajj*, there are also duties for *umrah*. These duties may be performed before or after the specific *hajj* dates. *Umrah* also includes *tawaf*, or walking around al-Ka'aba. In the course of my *hajj* and *umrah* in Mecca in 1991, I marched around al-Ka'aba dozens of times.

During the *hajj* and the days before and after, the Grand Mosque never sleeps. At any hour of the day or night you will find pilgrims circling al-Kaaba. During the day when the crowds are heavy, the sound of the voices is so loud that you can look at the person next to you and see his lips moving, but you cannot hear the words he is saying.

Chapter 5: An Unexpected Companion

Mustafa makes a reference to a woman being arrested for sitting with a male co-worker at a coffee shop. This actually happened to a thirty-seven-year-old woman from the United States who had come to Saudi Arabia with her husband. She was a managing partner of a finance company and was making a routine visit to some new offices. The electricity in the offices cut out, so she went with some of her male co-workers to Starbucks to use the wireless services. She and the male co-workers were sitting in a curtained booth reserved for families when she was arrested.[16]

---

[15] *Sahih Bukhari* (in Arabic), "Book of *al-Haj*," Kissing the Stone, no. 1597, and *The Correct Books of Bukhari* (in English), vol. 2, bk. 26, no. 679, http://www.usc.edu/dept/MSA/fundamentals/hadithsunnah/bukhari/026.sbt.html#002.026.679 (accessed September 2008).

[16] Sonia Verma, "Religious Police in Saudi Arabia Arrest Mother for Sitting With a Man," TimesOnline.com, http://www.timesonline.co.uk/tol/news/world/middle_east/article3321637.ece (accessed September 2008).

In this chapter, the story obviously takes a fictional turn as Mustafa meets a mysterious stranger. Yet the personality of this stranger is not a work of fiction. Whenever possible, I used information from Muhammad's life to inform Sheikh Ahmed's personality, habits, and reactions to the events that take place. For example, this chapter says that Sheikh Ahmed's favorite coffee is a latte sweetened with honey which is based on the fact that the hadith says Muhammad drank both milk and honey.

> Allah's Apostle was fond of honey and sweet edible things.[17]

In addition, Sheikh Ahmed was angry about how sites in Mecca were treated, but he did not raise his voice or become too emotional. This reaction is based on the following information.

> The Holy Prophet Muhammad said: "The best Jihad is self-control."[18]
>
> The Holy Prophet Muhammad said: "He is not strong and powerful, who throws people down, but he is strong who withholds himself from anger."[19]

Finally, this chapter describes the destruction of historic sites in Saudi Arabia, which is being carried out in reality.[20]

---

[17] Narrated Aisha, *The Correct Books of Bukhari* (in English), vol. 7, bk. 63, no. 193: http://www.usc.edu/dept/MSA/fundamentals/hadithsunnah/bukhari/063.sbt.html#007.063.193 (accessed September 2008).

[18] *Musnad Imam Ahmad bin Muhammad bin Hanbal* [*The Hadith of Ahmad ibn Hanbal*] (in Arabic) (Hockessin, Delaware: Noor Foundation International, 2005), hadith no. 22826.

[19] *Sunan Ibn Majah* (in Arabic), hadith no. 76, http://hadith.alislam.com (accessed September 2008).

[20] Zvika Krieger, "Mecca Bucks: Why Wahhabis Invited Starbucks to Islam's Holiest City," *The New Republic*, March 26, 2008, http://www.sunniforum.com/forum/showthread.php?t=32582. For specific information about Khadija's house, see "The House of Sayyida Khadija," *Islamica Magazine*, http://www.islamicamagazine.com/issue-15/the-house-of-sayyida-khadija.html.

Chapter 6: Better than Camels

The fictional Sheikh Ahmed wears scented oil just as Muhammad did. Aisha, Muhammad's young wife, said, "I used to perfume Allah's Apostle with the best scent available till I saw the shine of the scent on his head and his beard shine."[21]

The joke that Sheikh Ahmed told Mustafa came directly from the hadith:

> Anas said: A man came to the Prophet and said: O Apostle of Allah! give me a mount. The Prophet said: We shall give you a she-camel's child to ride on. He said: What shall I do with a she-camel's child? The Prophet replied: Do any others than she-camels give birth to camels?"[22]

Sheikh Ahmed made a subtle reference to *hijra* when he said, "I much prefer to make this journey by car during the day than by camel at night." *Hijra* is the Arabic word for the pivotal event in Islamic history when Muhammad emigrated from Mecca to Medina at night to escape his enemies. The Islamic calendar starts on this date, using the abbreviation A.H. to refer to "after *hijra*."

This chapter introduces a few Arabic words. For example, Mustafa asked Sheikh Ahmed a question about the *ummah. Ummah* is an Arabic word that refers to the Muslim community or nation. They also discussed the *burqa*, an outer garment that a Muslim woman wears over her daily clothing that covers almost all parts of a her body. The word *hijab* can refer generally to modest dress or more specifically to the head scarf or veil that Muslim women use to cover their hair and face or just their hair.

Sheikh Ahmed quoted Muhammad's warning to the people of

---

[21] Narrated Aisha in *The Correct Books of Bukhari* (in English), vol. 7, bk. 72, no. 806, http://www.usc.edu/dept/MSA/fundamentals/hadithsunnah/bukhari/072.sbt.html#007.072.806 (accessed September 2008).

[22] *Traditions of Abu Dawood* (in English), bk. 41, no. 4980, http://www.usc.edu/dept/MSA/fundamentals/hadithsunnah/abudawud/041.sat.html#041.4980 (accessed September 2008).

Mecca, "O people of Mecca, I swear in the name of Allah I come as a slaughterer."[23]

Mustafa asked Sheikh Ahmed whether women should still be covered. Here is the background story behind Sheikh Ahmed's answer. Muhammad married multiple wives in Medina, and he typically hosted a feast after each wedding. After the feast for Zainab bint Jahsh, several people lingered in his house after Muhammad left.[24]

The next day one of Muhammad's most trusted followers made this suggestion:

> Narrated Umar: I said, "O Allah's Apostle! Good and bad persons enter upon you, so I suggest that you order the mothers of the Believers (i.e. your wives) to observe veils."[25]

That same day Muhammad received the verse of Al-Hijab through the angel Gabriel.

> O Prophet! Tell your wives and your daughters and the women of the believers to draw their cloaks (veils) all over their bodies.That will be better, that they should be known (as free respectable women) so as not to be annoyed (Surah 33:59; see also verse 33 and Surah 24:31, 58ff, Muhsin Khan).

So Muhammad's wives and all the Muslim women had to cover themselves.

Finally, Sheikh Ahmed claimed that America has declared war on Islam, which is not true from America's point of view. But Sheikh

---

[23] Ibn Kathir (in Arabic), *The Beginning and the End*, vol. 2, pt. 3, p. 53.

[24] Ibn Ishaq, *The Biography of the Prophet* (in Arabic), 368.

[25] *The Correct Books of Bukhari* (in English), vol. 5, bk. 59, no. 447, http://www.usc.edu/dept/MSA/fundamentals/hadithsunnah/bukhari/059.sbt.html#005.059.313 (accessed September 2008).

Ahmed's mind-set is an accurate representation of the logic that is accepted by Muslim radicals.

Sheikh Ahmed spoke of Allah giving Muhammad permission to fight after he moved to Medina. This permission came in the form of the famous Quranic verse:

> And fight with them until there is no more persecution and religion should be only for Allah; but if they desist, then surely Allah sees what they do (Surah 8:39, Shakir).

What does this verse mean? It means Muslims would fight until two conditions were met: (1) their enemies stopped persecuting them, and (2) Islam was the only religion.

Now look at the last part of the verse, which reads: "if they desist, then surely Allah sees what they do." To understand the meaning of this phrase, simply read the verse preceding it:

> Say to the Unbelievers, if (now) they desist (from Unbelief), their past would be forgiven them; but if they persist, the punishment of those before them is already (a matter of warning for them) (Surah 8:38).

In other words, if the unbelievers stopped fighting and persecuting the Muslims and accepted Islam, then they would be forgiven for the things they did against the Muslims earlier. But if the unbelievers continued to fight and reject Islam, then the unbelievers would be punished as unbelievers were punished in the past.

You can read more about Muhammad's military strategy in Ibn Ishaq, *The Biography of the Prophet* (in English), translated by A. Guillaume, 16th printing (Karachi: Pakistan: Oxford University Press, 2003), 280ff. Muhammad led twenty-seven raids.[26]

---

[26] Ibn Kathir, *The Beginning and the End* (in Arabic), vol. 2, pt. 3, 659–660.

Chapter 7: The Mosque of the Prophet

In this chapter, Mustafa and Sheikh Ahmed visit the Mosque of the Prophet in Medina and the ancient cemetery next to it.

The first thing they did at the mosque was "pray two *raka'ahs*." A *raka'ah* is the standard unit of prayer that is used at every prayer time. A faithful Muslim will do these prayers five times a day for his or her entire life. Think about it: most people eat three meals a day, but the faithful Muslim will pray five times a day.

The prayer times are based on the rising and setting of the sun and the lunar calendar, so they vary according to season and location on the globe. For example, the prayer times for Cairo, Egypt, on August 19, 2008, were 5:00 a.m., 12:59 p.m., 4:34 p.m., 7:32 p.m., and 8:57 p.m. However, by August 31, the prayers started about an hour earlier, with dawn prayer at 4:09 a.m. and the night prayer at 7:41 p.m. Many websites will provide prayer times for specific locations and dates.

In this book, I will make reference to the prayers with English names, i.e. dawn (*fajr*), noon (*zuhr*), afternoon (*asr*), sunset (*maghrib*), and night (*isha*).

A Muslim prayer is very different from a Christian prayer. It is a scripted event that includes words, physical movement, and times for reciting small portions of the Quran. At one particular point in the prayer, the Muslim kneels with his or her forehead touching the ground; that is when he or she makes petitions to Allah. No matter what language you speak, the scripted part of the prayer and Quranic reciting is done in Arabic.

The prayers can be done almost anywhere, but it is preferable for men to pray in a mosque. Some mosques are better than others. In particular, Muhammad said that prayers in his mosque in Medina were worth one thousand times more than prayers anywhere else.[27]

In *Coffee with the Prophet*, I described the prayers that were significant to the story, which meant that some prayer times went unmentioned. However, it should be understood that Mustafa and Sheikh Ahmed were observant Muslims, and observed every prayer time as Islamic law required.

Mustafa described how Sheikh Ahmed walked quickly, while leaning forward as if he were walking downhill. One hadith says of Muhammad, "When he walks he walks inclining as if coming down from a height. I never saw a man like him before him or after him."[28]

Sheikh Ahmed's stories about Aisha all come from hadith and Islamic history. Here is a summary of those stories and their sources:

- Muhammad drinking from the cup after Aisha[29]
- Aisha throwing the plate of food on the floor[30]
- Gabriel turning his head when Aisha and Muhammad were in bed together[31]

The concept of a "mother in nursing" or a milk mother is well-known in the Muslim world.[32] The concept originated from an incident in

---

27 *Sahih Bukhari* (in Arabic), no. 1190, and *The Correct Books of Bukhari* (in English) vol. 2, bk. 21, no. 282, http://www.usc.edu/dept/MSA/fundamentals/hadithsunnah/bukhari/021.sbt.html#002.021.282 (accessed September 2008).

28 Ibn Sa'd, *Kitabh al-Tabaqat al-Kabir* [*The Highest Level*], as translated by S. Moinul and H.K. Ghazanfar (New Delhi: Kitab Bhavan, n.d.)

29 Al-Elbani, *Series of Correct Hadith* (in Arabic).

30 *Sahih Bukhari* (in Arabic), narrated by Anas.

31 *Sahih Muslim* (in Arabic), no. 2432 and *The Correct Books of Muslim* (in English) bk. 4, no. 2127, http://www.usc.edu/dept/MSA/fundamentals/hadithsunnah/muslim/004.smt.html#004.2127 (accessed September 2008); *Sahih Bukhari* (in Arabic) no. 3821.

32 Walaa Hawari, "Milk Kinship Can Be an Interesting Adoption Tool," *Arab News*, 7 September 2007, http://www.arabnews.com/?page=9§ion=0&article=100901&d=7&m=9&y=2007 (accessed September 2008).

the life of Muhammad. A family had adopted a boy named Salim before adoption was prohibited. He grew up as a part of their family, but after adoption was prohibited, he could no longer be alone in the house with his mother because he and his mother were no longer related. So Muhammad said that if the mother nursed the grown son five times, then he would be a son in nursing to her, and they could be alone in the same house. She did this.[33]

The history of the Al-Baqi Cemetery and the destruction of its historical landmarks are described on several websites.[34]

The story of how Muhammad's mother and father died comes from Dr. Huseyin Algul, "Aspects of His Life—Celebrating the Blessed Birth" (in English), March 22, 2006, http://www.infinite-light.org/content/view/8071/20/ and Muhammad ibn Abd al-Wahab, *The Biography of the Prophet* (in Arabic).

Chapter 8: A Mysterious Phone Call

This chapter describes how Mustafa and Sheikh Ahmed visited the grave of Muhammad's mother, near the city of Medina, Saudi Arabia. The incident is based on the following hadith:

> Abu Huraira reported: The Apostle of Allah (may peace be upon him) visited the grave of his mother and he wept, and moved others around him to tears, and said: I sought permission from my Lord to beg forgiveness for her but it was not granted to me, and I sought permission to visit her grave and it was granted to me. So visit the graves,

[33] *Malik's Muwatta* (in English), bk. 30, no. 30.2.12, http://www.usc.edu/dept/MSA/fundamentals/hadithsunnah/muwatta/030.mmt.html#030.30.2.12 (accessed October 2008)

[34] See the Al-Baqi article at islamicoccasions.com, http://www.ezsoftech.com/ISLAMIC/baqi.asp. Also see "Al-Baqi: The Madinah Cemetery" at Islamonline.net, http://www.islamonline.net/English/hajj/Landmarks/1425/10.shtml and Irfan Ahmed, "The Destruction of Holy Sites in Mecca and Medina," *Islamica Magazine*, http://www.islamicamagazine.com/Issue-15/The-Destruction-of-Holy-Sites-in-Mecca-and-Medina.html.

> for that makes you mindful of death.[35]

Muslims are taught to respect their mothers. They always quote Muhammad as saying, "Paradise is under the feet of your mother." Also, the hadith says a man came to Muhammad and asked, "Who deserves my obedience?" Muhammad answered, "Your mother." The man asked three more times, and Muhammad said "mother" each time, until he said "father" the last time.

Chapter 9: Suicide Shame

Sheikh Ahmed quoted an important hadith that condemns three forms of suicide: leaping from a mountain, drinking poison, or stabbing oneself.[36]

Sheikh Ahmed said Allah guarantees that the one who dies fighting jihad will enter Paradise. This concept is easily justified using the Quran and the hadith. A key verse is Surah 61:10–12:

> O ye who believe! Shall I lead you to a bargain that will save you from a grievous Penalty? That ye believe in Allah and His Messenger, and that ye strive (your utmost) in the Cause of Allah, with your property and your persons: That will be best for you, if ye but knew! He will forgive you your sins, and admit you to Gardens beneath which Rivers flow, and to beautiful mansions in Gardens of Eternity: that is indeed the Supreme Achievement (Ali).

This verse is further clarified by a story of a poor man who went to fight jihad with no intention of returning alive.

> While facing the enemy…the Messenger of Allah (may

---

[35] *The Correct Books of Muslim* (in English), bk. 4, no. 2130, http://www.usc.edu/dept/MSA/fundamentals/hadithsunnah/muslim/004.smt.html#004.2130 (accessed September 2008).

[36] Narrated Abu Huraira in *The Correct Books of Bukhari* (in English), vol. 7, bk. 71, no. 670, http://www.usc.edu/dept/MSA/fundamentals/hadithsunnah/bukhari/071.sbt.html#007.071.670 (accessed October 2008).

> peace be upon him) said: Surely, the gates of Paradise are under the shadows of the swords. A man in a shabby condition got up and said; Abu Musa, did you hear the Messenger of Allah (may peace be upon him) say this? He said: Yes. (The narrator said): He returned to his friends and said: I greet you (a farewell greeting). Then he broke the sheath of his sword, threw it away, advanced with his (naked) sword towards the enemy and fought (them) with it until he was slain.[37]

This story also supports the idea that a person who goes into battle expecting to be killed (a suicide bomber) will be rewarded with Paradise.

Muslim radical leaders who use suicide bombers must respond to the fact that Muslims are accidentally killed in the suicide bomb attacks. Ayman al-Zawahiri (second in command of Al-Qaeda) spoke to the issue in an internet article dated March 1996.

Al-Zawahiri told a story about a battle Muhammad led personally against Ta'if, a Jewish village near Medina. Muhammad commanded the army to use their weapons against everyone in the village—men, women, children, and the elderly. In another hadith, Muhammad had prohibited killing women and children, but when he attacked the city of Ta'if, he killed everybody inside. Al-Zawahiri wrote:

> At that time, women and children were there in the middle of the enemies, and there was no way to separate the enemies from them, so he had to kill all of them. This will give us light on the subject of killing the enemies of Islam who have Muslims in the middle of them. According to the law of Islam, it is one of the biggest sins for a Muslim to kill his Muslim brother, but if there is no way to kill the enemy without killing the Muslims in the middle of them, we should kill them and the enemies will go to hell

---

[37] Narrated Abdullah b. Qais, *The Correct Books of Muslim* (in English), bk. 20, no. 4681, http://www.usc.edu/dept/MSA/fundamentals/hadithsunnah/muslim/020.smt.html#020.4681 (accessed September 2008).

> and Muslims will go to Paradise.[38]

Reading this explanation, it's easy to understand how al-Zawahiri justified the attack on the World Trade Centers even though there were Muslims working in the Twin Towers that day.

Sheikh Ahmed complained about the fall of the Islamic caliphate. For thirteen hundred years, the Islamic caliphate was the political and spiritual organization that united Muslim lands. Most recently, the headquarters of the caliphate were in Turkey, but in 1924, Turkish President Kamal Ataturk established a thoroughly secular government and abolished the caliphate. It was as if the government of Italy abolished the Vatican. This event is considered a disaster by faithful Muslims worldwide, and a major goal of every Islamic radical group is to restore the caliphate.

Mustafa asked Sheikh Ahmed whether it was permissible for suicide bombers to kill women and children in their attacks. Sheikh Ahmed's answer came directly from the following two hadith.

> During some of the Ghazawat of the Prophet a woman was found killed. Allah's Apostle disapproved the killing of women and children.[39]

> The Prophet passed by me at a place called Al-Abwa or Waddan, and was asked whether it was permissible to attack the pagan warriors at night with the probability of exposing their women and children to danger. The Prophet replied, "They (i.e. women and children) are from them (i.e. pagans)."[40]

---

[38] Ayman Al-Zawahiri, *Healing the Breasts of the Believers*, Mark Gabriel's translation. The story of the capture of Ta'if is told in *Ibn Ishaq* (in English), 587–592.

[39] The Correct Books of Bukhari, vol. 4, bk. 52, no. 257, http://www.usc.edu/dept/MSA/fundamentals/hadithsunnah/bukhari/052.sbt.html#004.052.257 (accessed October 2008).

[40] Ibid., no. 256, http://www.usc.edu/dept/MSA/fundamentals/hadithsunnah/bukhari/052.sbt.html#004.052.256 (accessed October 2008).

Chapter 10: Enemies of Islam

Sheikh Ahmed complained, "America is only looking after her own interests. Her goal is still to destroy Islam through secular governments in the Muslim world." This opinion is false—America is not trying to destroy the religion of Islam. Nevertheless, Sheikh Ahmed's opinion is very real among Muslims today, especially radical Muslims.

Muhammad's response to the Battle of the Trench gives a clear picture of his attitude toward his enemies. The Battle of the Trench only resulted in a total of five casualties, only one of whom was a Muslim. Yet in response, Muhammad killed every man from the Jewish tribe of Banu Qurayzah—about seven hundred men.[41]

Abrogation: The key to understanding the Quran

In this chapter, Sheikh Ahmed explained, "When the Prophet lived in Mecca, he answered his enemies softly because Allah had not yet given him the ability to defend his religion. But after Muhammad moved to Medina, Allah gave him permission to fight his enemies. The new revelation of fighting cancelled out the older revelation of tolerance. This is a basic principle of understanding the Quran: the new cancels out the old." Sheikh Ahmed described the concept of abrogation, or *nasikh*, in Islamic theology. Abrogation simply means that newer revelations cancel out older revelations. The Quran says: "Whatever a Verse (revelation) do We abrogate or cause to be forgotten, We bring a better one or similar to it" (Surah 2:106, Muhsin Khan).

A good example of abrogation is the prohibition of alcohol. At first, Muslims were allowed to drink alcohol. Then Muhammad received a revelation saying that Muslims must not be drunk while praying, and finally Muhammad received a revelation saying all alcohol was prohibited. (See Surahs 2:219; 16:67; 4:43; 5:90.) In other words, the revelations about alcohol were progressive; the

---

[41] Ibn Hisham, *The Biography of the Prophet* (in Arabic), vol. 2, 193ff. See also Ibn Ishaq (in English), 450–465.

new ones replaced the old ones.

The principle of *nasikh* also applies to the treatment of non-Muslims. For example, Muhammad said in Mecca, "There is no compulsion in religion," meaning that a person cannot be forced to accept a religion (Surah 2:256). Muhammad also taught in Mecca that if Jews and Muslims rejected Islam, then the Muslims should just reaffirm that Muslims believe in Allah and leave the Jews and Christians alone (Surah 3:64). However, in Medina Muhammad said he received a revelation saying:

> Fight them until there is no more Fitnah (disbelief and polytheism, i.e., worshipping others besides Allah) and the religion (worship) will all be for Allah Alone [in the whole of the world]. But if they cease (worshipping others besides Allah), then certainly, Allah is All-Seer of what they do (Surah 8:39, Muhsin Khan).

This revelation did not confuse the Muslim community. They understood that in the past they would tolerate other beliefs, but now they would not. The new cancelled out the old. The revelation was progressive.

Chapter 11: The Afghani Man

The story of Abdul Rahman, an Afghani Muslim who converted to Christianity, made headlines around the world in 2006. Ultimately, Italy granted him asylum to protect him from the death penalty in Afghanistan.[42] The government of Afghanistan declared him mentally incompetent. This was probably a tactic to help the government appear to conform to Islamic law because a mentally incompetent person would not be held responsible for his actions.

Sheikh Ahmed said the blood of a Muslim could only be shed in three cases, one of which was apostasy, as the hadith explains:

---

[42] Associated Press, "Christian Convert Arrives in Italy," USAToday.com, March 29, 2006, http://www.usatoday.com/news/world/2006-03-29-convert-asylum_x.htm (accessed September 2008).

> Allah's Apostle said, "The blood of a Muslim who confesses that none has the right to be worshipped but Allah and that I am His Apostle, cannot be shed except in three cases: In Qisas for murder, a married person who commits illegal sexual intercourse and the one who reverts from Islam (apostate) and leaves the Muslims."[43]

Another hadith reports that Muhammad said, "Whoever changes his Islamic religion, then kill him."[44]

In the airport at Jeddah, Mustafa mentioned the miracle of the "moon splitting in half." This is a reference to a famous story about Muhammad splitting the moon in half.[45]

Siga is a real game that has been played in Egypt for thousands of years. For more information, see "Egyptian Siga: The Mother of All Board Games" at http://hem.passagen.se/melki9/Egyptian_Siga.htm.

Chapter 12: The *Amrad* Man

Amrad is the Arabic word for a man who has shaved his beard and moustache. In hadith, Muhammad said, "Cut the moustaches short and leave the beard (as it is)."[46] Muhammad's purpose was to distinguish the Muslims from the non-Muslims. Ibn Umar reported that Muhammad said, "Do the opposite of what the pagans do. Keep the

---

[43] Narrated Abdullah: *The Correct Books of Bukhari* (in English) vol. 9, bk. 83, no. 17, http://www.usc.edu/dept/MSA/fundamentals/hadithsunnah/bukhari/083.sbt.html#009.083.017 (accessed September 2008) and also *The Correct Books of Muslim* (in English), bk. 16, no. 4152.

[44] *The Correct Books of Bukhari* (in English), vol. 9, bk. 84, no. 57, http://www.usc.edu/dept/MSA/fundamentals/hadithsunnah/bukhari/084.sbt.html#009.084.057 (accessed September 2008).

[45] Surah 54:1; also, *The Correct Books of Bukhari*, vol. 6, bk. 60, no. 390, http://www.usc.edu/dept/MSA/fundamentals/hadithsunnah/bukhari/060.sbt.html#006.060.390 (accessed September 2008).

[46] *The Correct Books of Bukhari* (in English) vol. 7, bk. 72, no. 781 and *Sahih Bukari* (in Arabic), "Book of Clothing," no. 5892.

beards and cut the moustaches short."[47] Therefore, some Muslim scholars say that a person who has shaved his beard is violating the teachings of the Prophet and should not be permitted to lead prayers or teach in the mosque. (Note: The unshaven professor named Sheikh Hakeem is fictional.)

At the restaurant, Sheikh Ahmed did not read his menu to be consistent with the hadith says that Muhammad could not read or write.[48] Also, Sheikh Ahmed ordered lamb shoulder because hadith says that the shoulder was his favorite part of the lamb.[49]

It is true that an Egyptian policeman assaulted three Christian women who were trying to repair their church on August 25, 2008.[50] The story about Umm William and the policeman being suspended is fictional.

This chapter mentioned the fact that the Egyptian government freely allows new mosque construction but often hinders new church construction.[51]

Sheikh Ahmed said he liked a song with the lyrics, "I hate Israel, and I love Amr Moussa." This is a real song that is still popular all over the Arab-speaking world. Amr Moussa is an Egyptian leader who has been the secretary general of the Arab World League since 2001. The BBC news service reported in 2002:

> The Arab League's secretary-general may not be popular with Israel or the US, but Egyptians like him so much they literally sing his praises.

---

[47] *The Correct Books of Bukhari* (in English), vol. 7, bk. 72, no. 780 and *Sahih Bukari* (in Arabic), "Book of Clothing," no. 5891.

[48] *The Correct Books of Bukhari* (in English), vol. 9, bk. 87, no. 111 and vol. 1, bk. 1, no. 3.

[49] Ibn Ishaq (in English), 516, see also Ibn Hisham (in Arabic), vol. 2, pt. 4, 309.

[50] "Muslim Security Forces Assault and Beat Coptic Women Trying to Repair Church Floor," Dhimmi Watch, edited by Robert Spencer, http://www.jihadwatch.org/dhimmi-watch/archives/022368.php (accessed September 2008).

[51] U.S. Department of State, Egypt: International Religious Freedom Report 2005, Released by the Bureau of Democracy, Human Rights, and Labor, http://www.state.gov/g/drl/rls/irf/2005/51598.htm.

> Egypt's former Foreign Minister Amr Moussa was appointed to the top position in May of last year.
>
> Shortly before that, Egyptian crooner Shaaban Abdel Rahim released a hit song with the lyrics "I hate Israel and I love Amr Moussa."[52]

Chapter 13: A Disturbing Dream

Mustafa told Sheikh Ahmed that when he was a child, he saw a woman's decapitated body floating in one of the canals connected to the Nile River. When I was a child, I saw several bodies floating in canals at different times, usually women or girls. One day I actually saw men drag a young teenage girl to the edge of a canal and behead her, letting her head and body fall into the water. I was seriously traumatized by this scene and suffered violent nightmares afterward.

Chapter 14: The Faithful and the Unfaithful

The Israeli embassy in Egypt is at the top of a high rise to discourage attacks. The anti-Semitism of the Muslim world, including Egypt, cannot be denied. Every school child has heard the verses in the Quran that call Jews the children of monkeys and pigs (Surah 7:166, 5:60; 2:65). Even in a crisis of faith, a Muslim like Mustafa would have a hard time seeing past his anti-Semitism.

Sheikh Ahmed said the blood of a Muslim can only be shed in three cases: as punishment for murder, as punishment for adultery, and as punishment for leaving Islam.[53] Another hadith reports that Muhammad said, "Whoever changes his Islamic religion,

---

[52] Profile: Amr Moussa, January 23, 2002, http://news.bbc.co.uk/2/hi/middle_east/1766776.stm (accessed September 2008).

[53] Narrated Abdullah: *The Correct Books of Bukhari* (in English) vol. 9, bk. 83, no. 17, http://www.usc.edu/dept/MSA/fundamentals/hadithsunnah/bukhari/083.sbt.html#009.083.017 (accessed September 2008) and also *The Correct Books of Muslim* (in English), bk. 16, no. 4152

then kill him."[54]

The story about the Christian named Adi who went to see Muhammad comes from Sayyid Qutb, *Milestones Along the Road,* pages 107–108 (chapter 4). Sayyid Qutb (1906–1965) is a famous Egyptian radical whose writings are still very popular today. His books can easily be read in English on the internet at several sites, including the website for the Young Muslims of Canada.

Sheikh Ahmed compared Islamic law to Egyptian law for the issues of adultery, apostasy, slander, alcohol, and usury (charging interest). Some sources for current Egyptian law are in Arabic at the following websites:

- http://www.asharqalawsat.com/details.asp?section=17&issueno=8932&article=170441&feature=1 (adultery)
- http://www.yassar.freesurf.fr/library/bal556_07.html (apostasy and slander)
- http://www.yassar.freesurf.fr/library/bal556_07.html (alcohol)

Sheikh Ahmed said that Muhammad used to give Muslims forty lashes for drinking wine.[55]

Law of apostasy explained

Sheikh Ahmed ended his lecture by calling for enforcement of the laws of apostasy. The best explanation of the law of apostasy that I can give you is an excerpt from my book *Culture Clash* (Charisma House, 2007), pages 119–120.

Apostasy under Islamic law means a Muslim man or woman decides to leave Islam and go back to his or her previous religion or to believe in something else. Islamic law describes this crime as betraying the religion, and the Quran tells Muslims to "take them

---

[54] *The Correct Books of Bukhari* (in English), vol. 9, bk. 84, no. 57.

[55] Narrated Anas, *The Correct Books of Muslim*, bk. 17, no. 4230, http://www.usc.edu/dept/MSA/fundamentals/hadithsunnah/muslim/017.smt.html#017.4230 (accessed September 2008).

and kill them wherever ye find them."

> They long that ye should disbelieve even as they disbelieve, that ye may be upon a level (with them). So choose not friends from them till they forsake their homes in the way of Allah; if they turn back (to enmity) then take them and kill them wherever ye find them, and choose no friend nor helper from among them (Surah 4:89, Pickthal).

In context, it is clear that those who "disbelieve" in this verse are people who accepted Islam and then turned away. In the first part of the verse, the Muslim community is told to reject apostates as friends unless the apostates decide to leave their homes and rejoin the Muslim community. The second half of the verse says that if the apostates refuse to return to Islam, then the Muslims should "kill them wherever ye find them, and choose no friend or helper from among them."

Someone who has his own copy of the Quran may read verse 90 and say, "Dr. Gabriel, the Quran says that if the apostates don't fight the Muslims, then the Muslims shouldn't fight them. So maybe verse 89 only refers to killing apostates who fight Islam." My response is that Surah 4:90 only gives a small loophole of protection. Muhammad had entered into treaties with some groups who were not Muslim. If an apostate had belonged to one of those groups before he accepted Islam, he could return to that group and the Muslims would not kill him as long as he did not violate the terms of that treaty.

If there is any confusion about how to judge the apostate, then Islamic scholars look to the hadith. Muhammad said, "Whoever changed his Islamic religion, then kill him."[56]

A person who has left Islam gets a chance to avoid the death penalty by returning to his faith. First, the Muslim leader asks the

---

[56] *The Correct Books of Bukhari* (in English), vol. 9, bk. 84, no. 57, http://www.usc.edu/dept/MSA/fundamentals/hadithsunnah/bukhari/084.sbt.html#009.084.057 (accessed October 2008). Also see Ibn Majed (in Arabic), no. 2526.

person to repent and come back to Islam. If the person does that, there will be no punishment. But if he refuses, he has to be killed before the sunset of the third day.

Sheikh Ahmed quoted one of the most famous sayings of Muhammad: "If you see something done against Islamic law, you have to change it with your hand. And if you cannot change it with your hand, then change it with your tongue. If you cannot change it with your tongue, then you must change it with your heart. Changing it with your heart is the weakest stage of faith."[57]

Chapter 15: The Woman's Place

In this chapter, Sheikh Ahmed is a guest speaker for a class at Al-Azhar taught by one of Mustafa's friends, a liberal lecturer in the Islamic law faculty named Dr. Abdu (a fictional character).

When Dr. Abdu introduced the class, he mentioned that in Arab culture before Islam, some people killed their infant daughters as soon as they were born by burying them in the hot desert sand. The Quran mentioned this cruel practice in Surah 16:58–59:

> When news is brought to one of them, of (the birth of) a female (child), his face darkens, and he is filled with inward grief! With shame does he hide himself from his people, because of the bad news he has had! Shall he retain it on (sufferance and) contempt, or bury it in the dust? Ah! what an evil (choice) they decide on?

Dr. Abdu asked a variety of questions about women, which Sheikh Ahmed answered based on the Quran and the hadith. Most of the Quranic sources are listed in the main text of *Coffee with the Prophet*, but the hadith sources are listed below, organized by topic.

---

[57] *Sunan An-Nisai* (in Arabic), no. 4922.

- Women should not hold high government offices.[58]
- Women should clap in the mosque instead of speak.

> Then the Prophet said to the people, "If some problem arises during prayers, then the men should say, Subhan Allah!, and the women should clap."[59]

- Women must travel with a dhu-mahrum.[60]
- Women must speak more quietly than men when they are in the mosque, according to Malik's Muwatta, a collection of hadith compiled by scholar Malik bin Anas (93 A.H.–179 A.H.).

> Yahya related to me from Malik that he had heard the people of knowledge say, "Women do not have to raise their voices when they are doing talbiya, and a woman should only speak loudly enough to hear herself."[61]

- Women and men should be separated as much as possible. The late Sheikh Ibn Uthaimin, when asked if a woman was allowed to stand next to a man during prayer in the mosque, answered, "No, she can only stand behind him."[62] Sheikh Uthaimin hosted a popular radio program and taught at the Holy Mosque in Mecca for thirty-five

---

[58] Narrated Abdullah: *The Correct Books of Bukhari* (in English) vol. 9, bk. 83, no. 17, http://www.usc.edu/dept/MSA/fundamentals/hadithsunnah/bukhari/083.sbt.html#009.083.017 (accessed September 2008) and also *The Correct Books of Muslim* (in English), bk. 16, no. 4152.

[59] *Sahih Bukhari* (in Arabic), vol. 9, bk. 89, no. 300.

[60] *The Correct Books of Bukhari* (in English), vol. 3, bk. 29, no. 85, http://www.usc.edu/dept/MSA/fundamentals/hadithsunnah/bukhari/029.sbt.html#003.029.085 (accessed October 2008).

[61] *Malik's Muwatta* (in English), bk. 20, no. 20.8.35, http://www.usc.edu/dept/MSA/fundamentals/hadithsunnah/muwatta/020.mmt.html#020.20.8.35. See also *Malik's Muwatta* (in Arabic) no. 240, http://hadith.alislam.com.

[62] Arabic website http://woman.bdr130.net/1781.html.

years until his death in 2001.[63] He was considered a top authority on Islamic law.

- When men and women walk together, Muhammad said the women should walk behind the men.[64]
- Sheikh Ahmed quoted Muhammad as saying, "Be careful of the world and of women."[65] Muhammad also said that the first temptation the Israelites had was women, but there is nothing in Hebrew Scripture about this, and Muhammad gave no details about the nature of this temptation.
- The Quran says a Muslim man can marry a Jewish or Christian woman.

> The food of the People of the Book is lawful unto you and yours is lawful unto them. (Lawful unto you in marriage) are (not only) chaste women who are believers, but chaste women among the People of the Book, revealed before your time... (Surah 5:5).

Chapter 16: Daring Questions

In the story, I said that Sheikh Ahmed smiled rather than laughed at Sayid's jokes, to be consistent with Muhammad's personality. For example:

> ...(His Companions) would talk about matters (pertaining to the days) of ignorance, and they would laugh (on these matters) while (the Prophet) only smiled.[66]

---

[63] Saudi Gazette, January 12, 2001, http://www.fatwa-online.com/scholarsbiographies/15thcentury/ibnuthaymeen_whatthepaperssay.htm#2 (accessed October 2008).

[64] Dawud, Musnad, hadith #5272.

[65] Narrated by Abu Sayid Al-Kidri: *Sahih Muslim* (in Arabic), no. 2742 and *Sahih Tirmizi* (in Arabic), no. 2191. These can be accessed at the website http://www.olamayemen.com/html/, "The Salafi Scholars of Yemen" (in Arabic).

[66] *The Correct Books of Muslim* (in English), bk. 30, no. 5742, http://www.usc.edu/dept/MSA/fundamentals/hadithsunnah/muslim/030.smt.html#030.5742 (accessed October 2008; and *Sahih Muslim* (in Arabic), no. 1413.

The show *Daring Questions* is currently being aired by satellite to Arabic-speaking countries all over the world. The program is broadcast on Thursday evenings and is estimated to reach an astonishing number of viewers each week—one hundred and twenty million. I appeared as a guest on the programs that discussed the breastfeeding fatwa and the cartoon controversy as well as several other shows. We showed the cover of *Coffee with the Prophet* during one of the programs, and the responses that the producers received were nearly all positive. About nine out of ten people accepted the drawing. Only one out of ten was critical.

Dr. Ezzat Atiyah is a real professor who was a leader in the study of hadith at Al-Azhar for decades. He wrote the fatwa about women breastfeeding their male co-workers and was subsequently fired by the university for it. The episode was highly publicized and caused a major shock to people all over the Muslim world.[67] You can read the material used for the fatwa for yourself in a section of Malik's Muwatta titled, "Suckling of Older People," on the University of Southern California website.[68] The same hadith says that Aisha used breastfeeding to make it permissible to meet with particular men. For example, if she wanted to meet with a certain man, she would have her sister or a female cousin breastfeed him. Then that woman would accompany the man as he met with Aisha. Muhammad's other wives absolutely refused to follow this practice.

Even in the seventh century, many Muslims had trouble with a woman nursing an adult male. The Muslim community argued that Muhammad made a one-time indulgence for Salim's mother to make Salim her son by nursing. For everyone else, they said, a person can only become a son or daughter in nursing during the first two years of life. In short, breastfeeding an adult was as shocking in Muhammad's time as it is today.

---

[67] Associated Press, "Egypt: Fatwa Allows Breastfeeding Among Adults," May 21, 2007, http://www.jpost.com/servlet/Satellite?cid=1178708655924&pagename=JPost%2FJPArticle%2FShowFull (accessed September 2008).

[68] *Malik's Muwatta*, "Suckling of Older People," http://www.usc.edu/dept/MSA/fundamentals/hadithsunnah/muwatta/030.mmt.html#030.30.2.12

Chapter 17: The Apostates

The controversy about the cartoon drawings of Muhammad made headlines around the world.[69] After a plot to assassinate one of the cartoonists was uncovered, multiple Danish newspapers reprinted the cartoons in February 2008 to show their support for freedom of speech.[70]

The source for the Islamic law about insulting Muhammad is the highly respected medieval Islamic scholar Ibn Taymiyyah, in his book *The Sword on the Neck of the One Who Insults the Prophet*.[71]

Apostates from Islam have three days to repent and return to Islam and they will be forgiven. This tradition comes from Umar ibn al-Khattab, the second leader of Islam after Muhammad's death.

> Then Umar inquired, "Do you have any recent news?" He said, "Yes. A man has become a kafir after his Islam." Umar asked, "What have you done with him?" He said, "We let him approach and struck off his head." Umar said, "Didn't you imprison him for three days and feed him a loaf of bread every day and call on him to tawba that he might turn in tawba and return to the command of Allah?" Then Umar said, "O Allah! I was not present and I did not order it and I am not pleased since it has come to me!"[72]

On the *Daring Questions* television program, Dr. Mark Gabriel (me!) explained that insulting Muhammad had the harshest penalty

---

[69] BBC News, "Muhammad Cartoon Row Intensifies," http://news.bbc.co.uk/2/hi/europe/4670370.stm (accessed September 2008).

[70] BBC News, "Danish Muhammad Cartoon Reprinted," http://news.bbc.co.uk/2/hi/europe/7242258.stm (accessed September 2008).

[71] Ibn Taymiyyah, *As- Sarem al-Maslul ala Shatem al Rasul* [*The Sword on the Neck of the One Who Insults the Prophet*] (Beirut, Lebanon: Ibn Hazm Publishing, 1996).

[72] *The Correct Books of Muslim* (in English), bk. 36, no. 36.18.16, http://www.usc.edu/dept/MSA/fundamentals/hadithsunnah/muwatta/036.mmt.html#036.36.18.16 (accessed September 2008).

in all of Islamic law. Those who commit adultery can be forgiven for their sin through accepting their punishment, even though that might mean one hundred lashes or being stoned to death. For example, when a young adulteress was stoned to death, Muhammad commented, "She has made such a repentance that even if a wrongful tax-collector were to repent, he would have been forgiven."[73]

Islamic history gives detailed information about the assassination of Kaab ibn al-Ashraf, the Jewish poet who insulted Muhammad.[74]

Sheikh Ahmed said that Muhammad protected images of Mary, Jesus, and Abraham from being destroyed in al-Kaaba. The hadith says:

> After the conquest of Mecca] Apart from the icon of the Virgin Mary and the child Jesus, and a painting of an old man, said to be Abraham, the walls inside [Kaaba] had been covered with pictures of pagan deities. Placing his hand protectively over the icon, the Prophet told ‘Uthman to see that all other paintings, except that of Abraham, were effaced.[75]

The Union of Former Muslims is a real organization I founded in 2007. Its mission is "to defend the human rights of Muslims who have chosen to leave Islam and to provide them with a democratic, free environment where they can practice the right to choose their religion or beliefs." For more information go to http://shop.unionofformermuslims.com/main.sc or write to Union of Former

---

[73] *The Correct Books of Muslim* (in English), bk. 17, no. 4206, http://www.usc.edu/dept/MSA/fundamentals/hadithsunnah/muslim/017.smt.html#017.4206 (accessed October 2008).

[74] *The Correct Books of Muslim* (in English), bk. 19, No. 4436, http://www.usc.edu/dept/MSA/fundamentals/hadithsunnah/muslim/019.smt.html#019.4436.

[75] Martin Lings, *Muhammad: His Life Based on the Earliest Sources* (Rochester, VT: Inner Traditions International, Ltd., 1983), page 300, referencing al-Waqidi, Kitab al-Maghazi 834, and Azraqi, Akhbar Makkah vol. 1, p. 107, as quoted in "Muhammad and Idolatry" by Sam Shamoun and accessed at http://www.answering-islam.org/Shamoun/idolatry.htm.

Muslims, 2020 Pennsylvania Ave. NW, Box 681, Washington DC 20006, USA.

Sheikh Ahmed told how Abu Bakr fought the Muslims who refused to pay the *zakat*, or charity tax. These were known as the Ridda Wars, or the Wars of Apostasy. Abu Bakr sent Khalid ibn Walid to fight them, and he killed eighty thousand of these apostates in three months.

Chapter 18: Trapped

Sheikh Ahmed reprimanded Sayid for not praying and said that Sayid would crawl to prayer if he knew how important it was. The source for Sheikh Ahmed's attitude is this hadith:

> Muhammad said, "The heaviest prayer on the hypocrites [Muslim hypocrites] is the prayer of isha (night prayer) and the prayer of al-fajr (dawn prayer), and if they know what is in these two prayers, they will even crawl to them. And I almost commanded for the prayer to be started and another man to lead the prayer. Then I will go with another man with me carrying kindling wood and go to the people who did not come to the prayer and we will burn their homes with fire over them."[76]

Later, Sheikh Ahmed and Mustafa play a game of Siga on the roof of the house, a typical way to relax in Egyptian society. During their conversation, Sheikh Ahmed pressured Mustafa to be more committed to Islam.

Sheikh Ahmed reminded Mustafa that "dying as a martyr in jihad is your path to eternal life." Martyrdom is appealing in Islam because it is the only way to be sure of entering Paradise. Islam teaches that on Judgment Day a man's deeds are weighed, and then

---

[76] *Musnad Imam Ahmad bin Muhammad bin Hanbal* [*The Hadith of Ahmad ibn Hanbal*] (in Arabic), vol. 2, no. 367. See also, Narrated by Abu Haraira, *The Correct Books of Bukhari*, vol. 1, bk. 11, no. 617, http://www.usc.edu/dept/MSA/fundamentals/hadithsunnah/bukhari/011.sbt.html#001.011.617 (accessed October 2008)..

Allah decides if he may enter Paradise. If you live as an infidel, you may be sure of going to hell. But if you live the best Muslim life you possibly can, you still have no guarantee of entering Paradise. The hadith says:

> I heard Allah's Apostle saying, "The good deeds of any person will not make him enter Paradise." (i.e., None can enter Paradise through his good deeds.) They (the Prophet's companions) said, "Not even you, O Allah's Apostle?" He said, "Not even myself, unless Allah bestows His favor and mercy on me." [77]

There is only one guarantee for entering Paradise, and that is martyrdom while fighting jihad in the cause of Allah. The Quran says:

> Think not of those who are killed in the Way of Allah as dead. Nay, they are alive, with their Lord, and they have provision. They rejoice in what Allah has bestowed upon them of His Bounty, rejoicing for the sake of those who have not yet joined them, but are left behind (not yet martyred) that on them no fear shall come, nor shall they grieve. They rejoice in a Grace and a Bounty from Allah, and that Allah will not waste the reward of the believers (Surah 3:169–171, Muhsin Khan).

These verses were written specifically about participation in jihad, not about dying of other causes. In hadith, Muhammad clearly promised that a martyr's reward is Paradise.

> The Prophet said, "The person who participates in (Holy battles) in Allah's cause and nothing compels him to do so except belief in Allah and His Apostles, will be recompensed by Allah either with a reward, or booty (if he

---

[77] Narrated Abu Huraira, *The Correct Books of Bukhari*, vol. 7, bk. 70, no. 577, http://www.usc.edu/dept/MSA/fundamentals/hadithsunnah/bukhari/070.sbt.html#007.070.577 (accessed September 2008).

> survives) or will be admitted to Paradise (if he is killed in the battle as a martyr)."[78]

For more information, read my book *Journey Inside the Mind of the Islamic Terrorist* (Charisma House, 2006), especially chapter 11, "Faith Is the Reason."

Chapter 19: Family Crisis

The name of the family business, *Al-Rahal Fine Furniture*, and the type of business are fictitious.

Muhammad's son Ibrahim died when he was an infant, about 10 months old.[79]

The story of Mustafa's younger brother getting sunstroke has a strong connection to my own life. When I was in high school, I had a younger brother who went out to my family's garlic fields to help supervise the laborers. He spent the day in the hot sun and came home burning up with fever and desperately thirsty. My parents took him to the hospital, where he slipped into a coma. I was a young teen, and my parents would not allow me to see him while he was sick. He died in the hospital, and then I was permitted to come into the room to see his body for a few moments. I remember kissing his eyes and his cheeks before they made me leave. I was so distraught over my brother's death that I wanted to throw myself off the bridge over the river during his funeral procession.

Chapter 20: Explanations

In this chapter, Sheikh Ahmed reveals his identity to Mustafa and offers him various proofs that he is telling the truth.

---

[78] The Correct Books of Bukhari (in English), vol. 1, bk. 2, no. 35, http://www.usc.edu/dept/MSA/fundamentals/hadithsunnah/bukhari/002.sbt.html#001.002.035 (accessed September 28, 2005).

[79] *The Correct Books of Bukhari* (in English), narrated Anas bin Malik, vol. 2, bk. 23, no. 390, http://www.usc.edu/dept/MSA/fundamentals/hadithsunnah/bukhari/023.sbt.html#002.023.390.

Sheikh Ahmed reminded Mustafa that Allah would not allow any angel or spirit to appear in the image of Muhammad. This principle is well-known in the Muslim world and imams will talk about it during Friday sermons. It comes from the following hadith:

> He who sees my (description) after me, it is as if he had actually seen me, and he who sees it out of love and desire for me, God will forbid the fire of Hell to touch him. He will be safe from the trials of the grave, and he will not be sent forth naked on the day of resurrection.[80]

The ring

Sheikh Ahmed also showed Mustafa a silver ring as proof that he was the Prophet. The details about the silver ring, including the engraving and how it was lost in a a well, came directly from Islamic history. Here is the original story:

> ...When Abu Bakr became the Caliph, he wrote a letter to him (and stamped it with the Prophet's ring) and the engraving of the ring was in three lines: Muhammad in one line, "Apostle" in another line, and "Allah" in a third line. Anas added: "The ring of the Prophet was in his hand, and after him, in Abu Bakr's hand, and then in 'Umar's hand after Abu Bakr. When Uthman was the Caliph, once he was sitting at the well of Aris. He removed the ring from his hand and while he was trifling with it, dropped it into the well. We kept on going to the well with Uthman for three days looking for the ring, and finally the well was drained, but the ring was not found."[81]

---

[80] Al-Tirmizi, *The Prophet's Description* (in Arabic), no. 3623 and *Sahih Muslim* (in Arabic), no. 2266, http://78.129.135.138/?Cat=3&SID=5376 (accessed September 2008).

[81] Narrated Anas, *The Correct Books of Bukhari* (in English) vol. 7, bk. 72, no. 767, http://www.usc.edu/dept/MSA/fundamentals/hadithsunnah/bukhari/072.sbt.html#007.072.767 (accessed September 2008).

Speaking different languages

Sheikh Ahmed told Mustafa that Allah gave him the ability to speak "in any language I need in order to communicate with the believers." This idea comes from a story in hadith where the angel Gabriel gave Muhammad the ability to recite the Quran in seven different dialects.

> ...The Apostle of Allah (may peace be upon him) was near the tank of Banu Ghifar [when] Gabriel came to him and said: Allah has commanded you to recite to your people the Qur'an in one dialect. Upon this he said: I ask from Allah pardon and forgiveness. My people are not capable of doing it. He then came for the second time and said: Allah has commanded you that you should recite the Qur'an to your people in two dialects. Upon this he (the Holy prophet) again said: I seek pardon and forgiveness from Allah, my people would not be able to do so. He (Gabriel) came for the third time and said: Allah has commanded you to recite the Qur'an to your people in three dialects. Upon this he said: I ask pardon and forgiveness from Allah. My people would not be able to do it. He then came to him for the fourth time and said: Allah has commanded you to recite the Qur'an to your people in seven dialects, and in whichever dialect they would recite, they would be right.[82]

The most powerful verse of the Quran

Sheikh Ahmed told Mustafa: "Remember *Ayat al-Kursi*; it is the most powerful." Ayat al-Kursi literally means "the verse of the chair." This verse is well-known in the Muslim world and is recited as a prayer or as a means of protection. Muhammad said:

---

[82] Narrated Ubayy b. Ka'b, *The Correct Books of Muslim*, bk. 4, no. 1789, http://www.usc.edu/dept/MSA/fundamentals/hadithsunnah/muslim/004.smt.html#004.1789 (accessed September 2008).

> Whoever recites Ayat al-Kursi in the night before sleeping, Allah Most High will protect him, his house, and the neighbouring houses.[83]

Another well-known hadith about this verse is the following:

> Imam Muslim writes that Ubayy bin Ka'b narrated that one day, the Prophet asked "O Ubayy! What is the most excellent verse of the Quran?" Ubayy replied, "Allah and His Messenger know best." The Prophet said, "In your opinion, what is the most excellent verse of the Quran?" Ubayy bin Ka'b replied, "Allah – There is no god but He"(i.e. Ayat al-Kursi). The Prophet placed his hand on his chest and said, "O Ubayy bin Ka'b! May your knowledge be pleasant for you."[84]

As a result, when a Muslim is experiencing trouble, he will quote this special verse. The translation of *Ayat al-Kursi* in English that I used came from http://www.islamicinformationcentre.co.uk/alkursi.htm.

Chapter 21: A Dark Mosque

Mustafa was stunned by Sheikh Ahmed's revelations, but Mustafa focused on his brother, who had suffered sunstroke and was hovering between life and death at the hospital. Mustafa went to the mosque to pray for him and quoted a famous prayer from Muhammad: "I seek refuge in the perfect words of Allah from the evil of what he has created."

Muslims believe this prayer brings protection from harm because of the following hadith:

> A man who was stung by a scorpion was brought to the Prophet. He said: Had he said the word: "I seek refuge in

---

[83] *Tafsir al-Mazhari*, under the heading "Ayat al-Kursi. Qadi Thana'ullah Pani-pathi."

[84] Sharh Sahih Muslim: Fada'il al-Qur'an, under "Surat al-Kahf & Ayat al-Kursi." Allamah Ghulam Rasul Sa'idi.

the perfect words of Allah from the evil of what He created," he would not have been stung, or he said, "It would not have harmed him."[85]

Chapter 22: The Angel of Death Speaks

In this chapter, Mustafa thinks about the Islamic teachings about the afterlife as his brother's life fades away. Most of the Quranic sources are listed in the main text of *Coffee with the Prophet*, but the hadith sources are listed below, organized by topic.

- The angel of death speaks to the dying person.[86]
- The angel of death pulls the soul out of the dying person (Surahs 32:11; 6:61; 56:83; 79:1–2).
- A good Muslim's spirit will come out easily, like pouring out water.[87]
- The moment when the soul removed is described in more detail in the famous *Commentary on the Quran* (in Arabic) by al-Qurtubi (d. 1273 A.D. or 671 A.H.) in the chapter titled "The Taking of the Soul and the State of the Grave." This commentary is not fully translated into English, but volume 1 of the 10 volumes was published in English in 2003.

Chapter 23: Pray for Mercy

For a wealth of information about Muhammad and funerals, see book 23, titled "Funerals," *The Correct Books of Bukhari*, available online in English at the University of Southern California website.

During the funeral, Uncle Hamzi prayed, "O Allah, Forgive those of us that are alive and those of us that are dead; those of

---

[85] Narrated by Abu Hurayrah, *Sunan Abu Dawud* (in English), bk. 28, no. 3890, http://www.usc.edu/dept/MSA/fundamentals/hadithsunnah/abudawud/028.sat.html#028.3890 (accessed September 2008).

[86] http://forums.fatakat.com/archive/index.php?t-3914.html (in Arabic).

[87] Al-Qurtubi's commentary, al-Jamiu li Ahkam al-Quran, vol. 7, p. 42 in the section entitled "The Taking of the Soul and the State of the Grave."

us that are present, and those of us who are absent: those of that are young, and those of us that are adults; our males and females. O Allah! Whomsoever of us you keep alive, let him live as a follower of Islam, and whomsoever you cause to die, let him die as a believer." This prayer is always used at Muslim funerals because the hadith records Muhammad saying this prayer.[88]

Muhammad set an example of praying for the loved one at the gravesite.[89] Muslims hope Allah will respond to prayers for the dead. One hadith says:

> Allah's Apostle (may peace be upon him) used to say: The supplication of a Muslim for his brother at his back (in his absence) is responded so long as he makes a supplication for blessings for his brother and the commissioned Angel says: Amen, and says: May it be for you too.[90]

The source for the dead person saying "hurry" or "slow down" on the way to his grave is *Musnad Ahmad* (in Arabic), narrated Abu Huriara, vol. 2 p. 292, no. 7896.

Mustafa worried that two angels would be beating his brother in the grave as described in the following hadith: "In his grave, two angels will beat him with iron hammers between his ears."[91]

Chapter 24: Judgment Day

Muhammad said he did not know if he would spend eternity in

---

[88] *Sahih Tirmizi* (in Arabic). The English translation is from "A Guide for the Muslim Funeral," Islamic Society of North America, http://www.isna.net/Services/pages/A-Guide-for-the-Muslim-Funeral.aspx (accessed October 2008).

[89] *Sahih Sunan Abu Dawud* (in Arabic), vol. 2, p.620, no. 2758 and *The Hadith of Abu Dawud* (in English), bk. 20, no. 3196, http://www.usc.edu/dept/MSA/fundamentals/hadithsunnah/abudawud/020.sat.html#020.3196 (accessed September 2008).

[90] *The Correct Books of Muslim* (in English), bk. 35, no. 6590, http://www.usc.edu/dept/MSA/fundamentals/hadithsunnah/muslim/035.smt.html#035.6590 (accessed September 2008).

[91] *The Correct Books of Bukhari* (in English) vol. 2, bk. 23, no. 422, http://www.usc.edu/dept/MSA/fundamentals/hadithsunnah/bukhari/023.sbt.html#002.023.422 (accessed September 2008).

Paradise or hell.[92]

Mustafa's family hired a Quran reciter for the period of mourning because Muhammad said in the seventh century, "When you have a funeral for someone who has died, recite the Quran because the Quran is going to be his intercessor."[93]

Epilogue

Sheikh Ahmed was a character in a fictional story, but he represents the influence that Muhammad has around the world today. Like Muhammad, Sheikh Ahmed always kept his goal in mind: to protect and promote Islam. His interest in Mustafa centered around bringing him back to the faith and having him work to restore the caliphate through his position at Al-Azhar. Sheikh Ahmed also had contact with radical Muslim leaders around the world.

Sheikh Ahmed was charismatic and friendly to Mustafa at first. But as the days passed, he became more aggressive and critical. Mustafa was impressed by Sheikh Ahmed at first, but he soon became disenchanted with his critical attitude (especially at Al-Azhar). By the end of their time together, Mustafa was afraid of him. Sheikh Ahmed ultimately disappointed Mustafa, just as the Prophet of Islam ultimately disappointed me.

---

[92] Narrated Kharija bin Zaid bin Thabit, *The Correct Books of Bukhari* (in English), vol. 9, bk. 87, no. 145, http://www.usc.edu/dept/MSA/fundamentals/hadithsunnah/bukhari/087.sbt.html#009.087.145 (accessed September 2008).

[93] *Sahih Tirmizi* (in Arabic), vol. 4, no. 245.

Bibliography

The Correct Books of Bukhari (in English). Translated by M. Muhsin Khan. Available through the USC-MSA Compendium of Muslim Texts, http://www.usc.edu/dept/MSA/fundamentals/hadithsunnah/bukhari/.

Sahih Bukhari (in Arabic). Mecca, Saudi Arabia: The House of Revival of the Tradition of the Prophethood, 1978.

Traditions of Abu-Dawud (in English). Translated by Ahmad Hasan. Available through the USC-MSA Compendium of Muslim Texts, http://www.usc.edu/dept/MSA/fundamentals/hadithsunnah/abudawud/.

Ibn Hanbal, *Musnad Imam Ahmad bin Muhammad bin Hanbal* [*The Hadith of Ahmad ibn Hanbal*] (in Arabic). Hockessin, Delaware: Noor Foundation International, 2005.

Ibn Ishaq, *The Biography of the Prophet* (in English). Translated by A. Guillaume. Karachi: Pakistan: Oxford University Press, 16th printing, 2003.

Ibn Ishaq (or Ibn Hisham), *The Biography of the Prophet* (in Arabic). Cairo, Egypt: Al-Maktabah As-Salafiya.

Ibn Kathir, *The Beginning and the End*. Beirut, Lebanon: The Revival of the Arabic Tradition Publishing House, 2001.

Malik's Muwatta (in English). Translated by Aisha Abdarahman at-Tarjumana and Yaqub Johnson. Available through the USC-MSA Compendium of Muslim Texts, http://www.usc.edu/dept/MSA/

fundamentals/hadithsunnah/muwatta/.

The Correct Books of Muslim (in English). Translated by Abdul Hamid Siddiqui. Available through the USC-MSA Compendium of Muslim Texts, http://www.usc.edu/dept/MSA/fundamentals/hadithsunnah/muslim/.

Sahih Muslim (in Arabic). Riyadh, Saudi Arabia: Peace Publishing House, 1999.

Sunan Ibn Majah (in Arabic and English). Translated by Nasiruddin al-Khattab. Houston, Texas: Dar-us-Salam Publications, 2007.

Sayyid Qutb, *Milestones Along the Road*. Delhi, India: Markazi Maktaba Islami.

Sahih Tirmizi (in Arabic).

Ibn Taymiyyah, *As Sarem al-Maslul ala Shatem al Rasul* [*The Sword on the Neck of Those Who Insult the Prophet*].

Glossary

The glossary includes an informal pronunciation guide for words that are difficult to pronounce. The pronunciation guides are intended to improve ease of reading and do not reflect formal linguistic standards for phonetic spellings.

Aisha—Muhammad's second wife. She was six years old when they were engaged and nine years old when Muhammad consummated the marriage. She played a major role in the Islamic community before and after Muhammad's death.

A.H.—After *hijra*. The Islamic calendar starts in the year that Muhammad made the *hijra*, or emigration, from Mecca to Medina.

Al-Azhar—Oldest, largest, and most powerful Islamic university in the world based in Cairo, Egypt.

Allah—The God of Islam.

amrad—An Arabic term for a man who has shaved his beard and moustache.

apostate—One who renounces his religion.

apostasy, laws of—Islamic law regarding the treatment of an apostate from Islam.

Badr, Battle of—First battle of Muhammad in which he had a surprise victory over his rivals from Mecca inthe Valley of Badr.

Bakr, Abu—[*AW-bu BAW-kir*] Close companion of Muhammad, first caliph after Muhammad's death, father of Aisha (Muhammad's second wife).

Banna, Hassan al-—(1906–1949) Founder of the Muslim Brotherhood, the grandfather of all modern Muslim radical groups.

al-Baqi Cemetery—Ancient cemetery next to the Mosque of the Prophet in Medina, Saudi Arabia. The cemetery contains the graves of Muhammad'swives, closest companions, and many other early Muslims.

Bedouin—Member of a desert-dwelling tribe.

Black Stone—Muslims believe the Black Stone fell to earth to show Abraham where to build a temple to Allah. The Black Stone is now imbedded in a corner of al-Ka'aba.

burqa—A large outer garment that covers almost all parts of the body. Muslim women wear the *burqa* over their daily clothing when they are outside of the home or with non-family members.

caliph—An Arabic word that means "leader." The term caliph specifically refers to the successors of Muhammad who served as the political and spiritual heads of Islam.

caliphate—The "office or dominion" of the caliph. The last caliphate (the Ottoman Empire) was based in Turkey until its fall in 1924.

dhu-mahram—A woman's husband or a man that she cannot marry according to Islamic law, such as her brother or father-in-law. Islamic law says that a woman must be accompanied by a *dhu-mahram* when she travels.

Fatima—Muhammad's favorite daughter.

Gabriel—The name of the angel that Muhammad said revealed the words of the Quran to him.

Grand Mosque—The mosque in Mecca where al- Ka'aba is located. In Arabic it is called *Al- Masjid al-Ḥarām,* or "the Sacred Mosque."

hadith *[ha-DEETH]*—The record of Muhammad's words and actions. This material was committed to memory for several generations and then collected and recorded by Muslim scholars. The most reliable collections were put together by al-Bukhari (A.H. 194–256) and Muslim (A.H. 202–261).

hajj—A pilgrimage to Mecca performed by observant Muslims at least once during a lifetime if possible.

hajji—A Muslim who has completed the *hajj.*

Hassan ibn Ali—One of Muhammad's grandsons. He tried to take over leadership of the Muslim state, but he was poisoned by his rival Muawiyya.

Husayn ibn Ali—One of Muhammad's grandsons. He was killed by Muawiyya's son Yazid.

hijab—A woman's veil or head scarf.

hijra—Arabic name for the pivotal point in Islamic history when Muhammad fled from persecution in Mecca and relocated to Medina.

imam—An Islamic leader, usually in charge of a mosque.

Islam—The religion founded by Muhammad. Its beliefs are based on the Quran and the life of Muhammad.

Islamic law—Called ***sharia*** in Arabic, Islamic law is first based on the Quran and then the hadith. For issues not specifically addressed by those sources, scholars rely on consensus, analogy, and precedent. Islamic law covers a broad range of public and private aspects of life, including hygiene, sexuality, what to eat and drink, banking laws, and criminal law (for murder, robbery, etc.).

jihad—Holy war; fighting those who resist Islam.

Judgment Day—According to Islamic teaching, on this day all human beings—both dead and living—will go before Allah to be judged.

al-Ka'aba—Literally meaning "the cube" in Arabic, this is the cube-shaped building in the courtyard of the Grand Mosque in Medina. Imbedded in a corner of al-Ka'aba is the famous Black Stone, which Muslims believe fell from heaven to show Abraham where to build a house of worship to Allah.

Khattib, Umar ibn al-—Second leader of the Islamic state after the death of Muhammad.

Mecca—Birthplace of Muhammad and place where he first received Quranic verses from the angel Gabriel. Located in present-day Saudi Arabia.

Medina—The city in present-day Saudi Arabia where Muhammad established his government and lived for eleven years until his death.

Mina—A small, uninhabited village east of Mecca. During the *hajj*, large tent cities at Mina house thousands of pilgrims. This is where the stoning of Satan takes place on the last day of the *hajj*.

Mount Arafat—Also known as the Mount of Mercy. A mountain near Mecca (in present-day Saudi Arabia) where Muhammad preached his final sermon during the *hajj*.

Mosque of the Prophet—Also called *Al-Masjid al-Nabawi*, or the Prophet's Mosque. It is located in Medina and holds the site of Muhammad's grave.

mother in nursing—According to Islamic law, after a woman nurses a child, she becomes the child's "mother in nursing." This means that the woman may spend time alone with the child as if the child were her own.

Muawiyya—Founder of the Umayyad Dynasty. He is believed to have poisoned Muhammad's grandson Hassan ibn Ali, who was trying to take over leadership of the Islamic state.

Muhammad—(A.D. 570 to 634) Founder of Islam.

Muslim—A person who practices Islam.

nasikh—The principle of continuing revelation in the Quran. In the case of a contradiction, newer teachings abrogate, or cancel, older teachings.

People of the Book—The phrase used in the Quran and hadith to refer to Jews and Christians because they received holy books from God.

Prophet of Islam—The typical way Muhammad is referred to by people in the Muslim world. Muhammad is often called simply "the Prophet."

Ottoman Empire—Muslim caliphate lasting from A.D. 1301–1924.

Quran—The words of Allah revealed to Muhammad in seventh-century Arabia. The Quran is 114 chapters long—about the length of the Christian New Testament.

Quraysh—Powerful governing tribe of Mecca at the time of Muhammad's birth. Muhammad's father was a member of this tribe.

Qurayzah—Jewish tribe that Muhammad put under siege and then captured. Muhammad killed all the men and took the women and children as prisoners.

Qutb, Sayyid—(1906–1965) [*SAH-yeed KOO-tib;* OO as in foot] A key leader of the twentieth- century radical Muslim movement. Of all radical writings, his are the most widely read and circulated, particularly his book *Ma'alim fi'l Tariq* [*Milestones Along the Road*], for which he was executed by the Egyptian government in 1965.

raka'ah—A unit of prayer according to Islamic teaching. A Muslim will perform two or more *raka'ahs* at each of the five daily prayer times.

Ramadan—Islamic holy month during which Muslims fast from food and liquids between the first and fourth prayers of the day.

rightly guided caliphs—The four rightly guided caliphs were the four successive leaders of the Muslims state after the death of Muhammad. In order of succession, they were Abu Bakr, Umar ibn Al- Khattib, Uthman bin Affan, and Ali ibn Abu Talib.

sharia—See Islamic law.

sheikh—A term of reverence for an ordained religious leader in Islam.

Shiite, Shia—One of the two major Islamic sects; in early Islamic history the Shia followed Ali ibn Abu Talib as the successor of Muhammad.

Siga—An Egyptian board game that dates back approximately three thousand years but is still played in Egypt today.

sunnah—The words and actions of Muhammad, the prophet of Islam. The record of these words and actions are called hadith.

Sunni—One of the two major Islamic sects; in early Islamic history the Sunni followed Muawiyya as the successor of Muhammad.

surah—The Arabic word for "chapter" in the Quran.

tawaf—To walk around al-Ka'aba seven times in a counter-clockwise direction as part of the *hajj* or *umrah* ritual.

Taymiyyah, Ibn—(A.D. 1268–1328) [*Ib-in tie-MEE- yuh*] A conservative Islamic scholar who is often quoted by radicals. He called for Muslims to fight jihad against the Mongols who had conquered the Islamic caliphate.

Umayyad Dynasty—Muslim caliphate founded by Muawiyya, which lasted from A.D. 661 to 751 (A.H. 41 to132).

umm—Arabic word meaning "mother of." It is often used as part of a woman's name, i.e. Umm William, "mother of William."

ummah—The Muslim community or nation.

umrah—Sometimes called the lesser pilgrimage, it is a set of rituals in

Mecca that may be performed at any time of the year. *Umrah* may be combined with a *hajj* pilgrimage or done separately. The rituals include circling al-Ka'aba, walking seven times back and forth between the hills of Safa and Marwah, and shaving or trimming the hair.

usury—Charging interest for loans.

Yazid—Son of Muawiyya, founder of the Umayyad Dynasty. He ordered the murder of al-Husain, Muhammad's grandson.

Index of Quranic References

Author's Academic Credentials

Dr. Gabriel's academic credentials in Islamic scholarship include:

- Bachelor's, master's, and doctorate degrees in Islamic history and culture from Al-Azhar University, Cairo, Egypt
- Graduating second in his class of six thousand students for his bachelor's degree. This ranking was based on cumulative scores of oral and written exams given at the end of each school year.
- One of the youngest lecturers ever hired at Al-Azhar University. He started lecturing after he finished his master's degree and was working to finish his doctorate.
- Traveling lecturer. The university sent him to countries around the Middle East as a lecturer in Islamic history.

Al-Azhar University is the most respected, authoritative Islamic university in the world. It has been in continuous operation for more than one thousand years.

In addition to his academic training, Dr. Gabriel had practical experience, serving as the imam at a mosque in the Cairo suburbs.

Interested in More Books by Dr. Gabriel?

Learn more about the teachings of Islam from one who lived it for thirty-four years.

Islam and Terrorism

Learn what the Quran teaches about violence and the goals of Islamic jihad. It also tells about Dr. Gabriel's astounding journey from lecturing at Al-Azhar University to seeking religious asylum in the United States. (2002)

Islam and the Jews

Find out the role of Islam in the clash between Israel and the Muslim world. It exposes what the Quran and Muhammad taught about Jewish people. (2003)

Jesus and Muhammad

Walk through the lives of the two influential figures of history and discover similarities that will amaze you and contradictions that will make you think. This book holds surprises for both Christians and Muslims. (2004)

Journey into the Mind of an Islamic Terrorist

Get inside the mind of an Islamic terrorist. This book exposes the frightening logic behind groups like Al-Qaeda and HAMAS. (2006)

Culture Clash

Discover what it would be like to live under Islamic law in this eye-opening exposé of the difference between Islamic culture and modern culture. (2007)

Place your order at www.coffeewiththeprophet.com,
www.gabrielpublishing.org,
or wherever fine books are sold.